Ali the Canary. A Barbary corsair

Moisés Morán Vega

Published by Ediciones Doble A, 2024.

While every precaution has been taken in the preparation of this book, the publisher assumes no responsibility for errors or omissions, or for damages resulting from the use of the information contained herein.

ALI THE CANARY. A BARBARY CORSAIR

First edition. July 5, 2024.

ISBN: 979-8227756411

Written by Moisés Morán Vega.

Table of Contents

The Souls and the Journey

On the morning of July 26th, 1655, the brigantine "The Souls" was docked at the Las Palmas pier. That very day, it would set sail for Barbary. Captain Juan Sánchez was giving the final check to the provisions, rigging, gear, sails, and oars. He also ensured that they had enough supplies for over forty days of fishing near the African coast.

Captain Sánchez was an experienced fisherman. He had been fishing along the coasts of Africa for over twenty years, starting as a child with his father, from whom he learned the trade and its secrets. However, in recent years, fishing had become a risky endeavor. Pirates and corsairs from Algiers had greatly harmed the fishing activity in the islands. There was no other choice but to head to the fish banks abundant near Cape Bojador. This was the only activity that brought in some money to support his family.

Fishing was one of the main economic activities for the citizens of Las Palmas, upon which many families depended. Salted fish was also a staple food in the Canarian diet and the main product that ship captains bought when they stopped at the port on their way to America or Africa, as it preserved very well.

Gran Canaria boasted a magnificent anchorage known to seafarers, the bay of Las Isletas, which served as a natural refuge for ships bound for the New World or Africa, allowing them to rest and stock up on fresh produce such as fruit, vegetables, water, oil, or salted fish, through the multitude of auxiliary boats that approached the anchored vessels.

The city of Las Palmas also had a dock, barely three hundred meters long, which served as the gateway to the city, although it was small and poorly located. Only a few ships could dock there, and when the southerly winds blew strong and the black flag was raised due to the dreaded "rebosos," it was impossible to carry out loading and unloading operations, forcing ships to seek refuge in the shelter of Las Isletas bay.

Fishing was big business, and a successful campaign could yield a substantial amount of money, ensuring more than six months of financial security. Many Canary Islanders ventured to embark despite the dangers it entailed.

One of the chief concerns of the masters was salt; without it, they couldn't set sail. This raw material was essential for the salting of fish, which was done at sea.

For this reason, Captain Juan Sánchez had visited the Bufadero Saltworks in Bañaderos the day before. On this occasion, he had negotiated the purchase of 300 bushels of salt, which he would guard like gold in his holds.

The price of salt was a source of dispute between salt workers and sailors, and this time was no different. Upon arriving at the saltworks, the boatswain, a trusted man of the master, disembarked to negotiate the price with the salt worker, agreeing not to pay more than 980 maravedis per bushel.

The boatswain approached a landing stage with a skiff. He disembarked and headed to meet the salt worker, a gaunt man so dark that he seemed mulatto. He was dressed in clothes that were once white but had turned yellowish due to the sun's action.

He recognized him instantly because he had done business with him on other occasions. He was talking to one of his employees. He raised his head, approached Benjamín, and asked:

"Are you here to buy salt?"

"Yes, a bushel."

"You know the price has skyrocketed. There is much demand at the beginning of the fishing season."

"The price never goes down. When it's not one thing, it's another," complained the sailor. "I offer you 880 maravedis per bushel. Not a penny more, not a penny less."

The salt worker considered the offer the fisherman was making. He knew the bargaining game was about to begin.

"For that price, we have little to discuss, sailor. You need the salt, and I need your money. 990 is the price at which I'm selling the bushel."

"990? That's robbery. 930, and we close the deal."

"This is not robbery, my good sir. It's the price. I can leave it at 980, and I'm losing money."

"960, neither for you nor for me, what do you say? My captain is willing to go to the southern saltworks, even if we lose a day, there we'll surely be able to buy salt at a cheaper price."

The salt worker took a pinch of salt with his hand, thinking the sailor might be right. He knew that salt prices in the south were much cheaper, but he also knew that few captains risked going there because the strong winds prevailing in that area made loading salt very difficult.

"So, what do you say, old man? Do we close the deal at 960 maravedis?"

"For this time, I'll accept, but next season, I won't be so lenient."

The boatswain smiled, shook his hand, and said, "Deal. We'll send some sailors to start loading the bushels of salt. I'll go to the ship to get the money to pay you the agreed price."

The boatswain took the skiff and returned to the ship to deliver the good news to the captain.

As he boarded, the captain asked, "How did the operation go?"

"Well. Do you know these salt workers seem like Moors? They spend all day bargaining over a damn bushel of salt. In the end, I closed at 960 maravedis per bushel."

"Very good. You're a skilled negotiator, bargaining like a Jew, Benjamín. Remind me to reward you with a score of snappers when we finish the salting."

"With this one, you have to be very careful because he has a very bad temper, sir."

"I know, it's not the first time he's called us Jewish usurers. He just lacks throwing stones at us. Every time we come to buy salt from him, we have to haggle over the price, but that's the game; sometimes you win, and sometimes you lose."

"He told me that this time he'd let it pass, but that for the next season, he wouldn't negotiate the price and that it would be a fixed price."

"At least we have the salt we need to salt all the fish, and that's the most important thing. You know that without salt, we can't set sail. So I'm very happy. When we have them in the holds of our ship, we'll set sail without delay."

The boatswain ordered ten sailors to get to work loading the bushels of salt they had purchased on board and then accompanied them to make the previously agreed payment.

After a few hours of hard work at the saltworks, they returned to the port of Las Palmas. Once there, the captain counted the sailors under his command. On board, he only had fifteen, and to carry out the fishing campaign successfully, he needed at least seventeen men. The captain and the boatswain were aware of the difficulty of finding sailors willing to embark on a fishing boat bound for the coasts of Africa. They knew that corsairs roamed those shores, and if they were unlucky enough to be captured, their fate was nothing other than being sold as slaves in any square in Algiers. However, they also knew about the need of many families, and their last resort was to embark on a fishing boat to bring in some money for the family's livelihood, which often meant the survival of the offspring for a year.

Simón Romero Arráez

Simon was born in 1639 on Triana Street in Las Palmas, into a humble family like many that populated the neighborhoods of 17th-century Canary Islands.

The idea of enlisting on a fishing boat came from his father, who saw no way out of the family's dire economic situation unless they had some help from their descendants. He couldn't count on his three daughters, who were of marrying age and already had arranged marriages. His eldest son, Gaspar, had gone to the New World; and the next one, Salvador, was learning the trade of ship carpentry, leaving only Simon, who was sixteen at the time. He had no known trade or benefit and spent most of his time playing with his friends, fishing on the pier, and loafing around the streets of the city.

One day, before lunch, his father called him in a very serious tone:

"Yesterday, I heard at the pier that they are looking for sailors to go fishing in Barbary. Some extra coins would come in handy for our family. I think you're old enough to join a crew and become a good sailor. They say they pay well, and as you gain experience, the salary will be much higher. Our situation here gets worse every day. My salary barely covers enough food for all of us. We have no other way out."

"I don't know, father. I'm fine here, and I wouldn't like to go on a fishing boat. They say many who embark never return, that the Moors capture them, then sell them as slaves, and they end up rowing in the galleys until they die."

His father, Juan Romero, was aware of the dangers they faced on those coasts. A considerable number of fishing boats had been captured by the corsairs sailing the Mediterranean and the Berber coast. Many had not returned, as they had been sold as slaves in Algiers or Turkey. But the need was greater than the dangers they might face on those coasts because a good catch guaranteed economic security for months.

"I know, son, but you know we need the money you could earn if you join that boat. We barely have enough to eat here. As you spend your days playing in the streets, you don't realize how bad things are. The money you could earn on that fishing boat would be very helpful for us."

The boy fell silent. He couldn't understand what his father was telling him, and it was true; he was very oblivious to domestic and family matters.

"Father, I'm scared. You don't know the things they say about the Moors and what they do with the slaves they capture."

"Simon, I know you're taking a risk, but I need you to board that fishing boat. There's no other way," he said categorically.

Juan Romero knew his son was right, that there was a good chance he would never return home if he boarded the fishing boat and that he would lose a son. However, it was a risk that had to be taken, albeit reluctantly and with a heavy heart.

"Tell me where that boat is, father, and who I need to talk to," he said resignedly.

"The brigantine is docked at the pier and is called 'The Souls.' When you get there, ask for Captain Juan Sanchez; he will explain the details to you. I hope you make it on time."

Simon left with his head down and walked the streets of Las Palmas with tired steps. He hoped his father would come out and yell at him not to go, that he had changed his mind, but that yell never came.

He hoped that when he reached the port, the ship would have already sailed. But upon arriving at the shipyards on Triana Beach, he spotted the only ship moored at the pier to the north. That must be the one his father had mentioned. He walked along the beach until he reached the pier. He walked slowly until he reached where the sailboat was docked. He observed it carefully. It was a large ship, with two masts and two square sails fluttering in the wind. There were sailors moving back and forth on the deck, and others were boarding a multitude of goods through a wooden gangway that connected the pier to the ship. Among the articles, he distinguished fresh fruit, water, and vegetables.

He stood in front of the boat for a moment. He intended to turn around and tell his father that he had been told they had the quota of sailors filled, but he didn't. He knew his family needed him to board that ship. Part of his family's future depended on him.

The boatswain asked him from the bow:

"What are you looking at, cabin boy?"

"I was looking for Captain Juan Sanchez. I would like to know if they still accept sailors," said Simon, almost embarrassed.

"You've arrived just in time. We have one spot left to complete the crew. Wait while I call Master Juan."

Simon waited on the edge of the pier, watching the maneuvers of the sailors on the deck. A tall, dark, thin man with a beard and a black woolen cap came out from inside. He approached the starboard side, grabbed one of the ropes holding the mast, and approached Simon:

"I'm Captain Juan Sanchez. How old are you?"

"Sixteen, sir, but you could say I'm seventeen because I'll turn seventeen later this year."

"Do you want to enlist as a sailor? This is very hard work, men's work, and once we set sail, there's no turning back."

The young man thought about telling him no, that he didn't want to board his ship, that all he wanted was to run back home and continue with the life he had lived until then.

"Yes, yes, I want to be a sailor," he said without much enthusiasm and lying through his teeth.

"Something tells me you don't want to much, but I'm not going to argue with you about that. If you say you want to be one of my crew, I believe you."

"Thank you, sir."

"We set sail tomorrow after sunrise. Come before eight. Now go to your house and eat something; then bring some clothes and don't forget your coat. You'll need it. Nights are very cold at sea, and the humidity gets into your bones."

"I'll be here, sir," he said hesitantly.

"We'll wait for you, cabin boy, and prepare yourself for hard work."

Simon turned around and headed for his house

. He smiled for the first time. He liked Captain Sanchez, and in a way, the short conversation with him had changed his mind. He quickened his pace until he began to run like crazy towards his house.

Upon arriving, he shouted from outside:

"Father, father, they accepted me, I'm a sailor!"

His father came out to greet him and, smiling, said:

"It's good news, son, very good. You don't know how happy I am. Your work will be very helpful for us."

"The captain told me we're leaving tomorrow and that I have to be here before eight in the morning. I have to bring clothes and a coat because it's very cold at sea."

His father knew very well that it was cold at sea because he had embarked three times as a temporary sailor on a coastal fishing boat.

"Don't worry about that. Your mother has your clothes ready; she'll even give you a woolen cap she made for your brother Gaspar, but he forgot it when he left for the Americas."

"Thank you, father."

"I see you're happier."

"Yes, I like the captain, he seems like a good person."

"That makes me happy, that you're encouraged. Well, let's eat, sailor."

Juan Romero was happy because his son had secured a place on the fishing boat. However, he felt pressure in his chest because he knew he was sending his youngest son into the lion's den, but there was no other way. The family needed that money, and the risk had to be taken.

That same night, his wife revived the unease he felt by asking:

"Juan, are you sure you're sending Simon to Barbary? Do you know what they say out there?"

"I have ears too, Maria, and I know what is said in the corners of this city. I know someone who has a son imprisoned in Algiers, but there's no other remedy. You know how we are. We need that money like water in May."

The situation in Gran Canaria was untenable. Most of the population lived in abject poverty, and fishing was one of the sources of income available to Canary families.

"Why don't you send Salvador then?"

"Salvador is learning a trade, and when he finishes, he can help us a bit."

"Yes, but while he's doing it, not even a miserable coin enters this house. He's the one who should board that ship, and Simon should learn the trade of ship carpentry."

"And what do you think I've done? I talked to Salvador, but he said no, that he was fine as he was and that he almost learned the trade of ship carpentry. What else can I do, Maria?"

His wife remained silent and then said:

"I didn't know you had talked to Salvador. You never tell me anything. Even so, I don't like Simon boarding. He's our little one, Juan, our little son, and we're sending him almost to the end of the world."

"I know, woman, but our son is a smart, strong, and very brave boy. You know he can defend himself well. Don't worry; he'll get through this."

"Yes, but if those Moors capture him, what are we going to do, Juan?"

Juan Romero knew that if he were captured, they could never pay the ransom, and they would lose him forever. Even so, he said:

"Don't think about that, Maria, let's go to sleep, tomorrow will be a very hard day. Please go to sleep."

Juan Romero hardly slept that night because anxiety ate him up inside. He was the first one who didn't want his youngest son to board the fishing boat; he would even change places with him, but he already had a stable job, and it was the only salary that entered their house.

The decision was made. His son Simon would leave the next day for the coasts of Africa.

The Departure

Simón woke up early and walked to the Triana beach, which was just a few meters from his house. From there, he could clearly see the Las Ánimas boat, which would be his temporary home for one to two months. He sat on the shore and watched the sunrise as the sun made its way over the horizon, claiming to be the sole owner of the new day.

He looked at his hands, they were a little sweaty. He felt a pressure in the pit of his stomach, a sensation he had never experienced before. Yes, he was very nervous because he had never been off Gran Canaria, and this would be the first time he left the island where he was born.

Inside him, he harbored mixed feelings. On one hand, he was eager to embark on this new adventure, but on the other hand, he didn't want to leave his island, leave behind the world he knew, his family, and his friends. This part was the one he liked the least.

He got up, picked up a flat stone, and threw it into the sea as his brother Gaspar had taught him. The pebble skipped five times over the water before finally sinking.

He turned his head at the sound of someone approaching. There was his father, smiling at him, asking:

"How did you sleep?"

"Well, although I was already awake before dawn."

"What's bothering you, Simón?"

"Nothing, father, I'm just nervous. For me, this situation is new. You know I've never left this island, not even this city. My life is here, I don't know anything beyond what my eyes can see. It's just that, leaving the life I know for a few months is something I don't like very much."

"I know, son. You know we have no choice but to send you to the coast. We need that money to get our heads above water. Do you understand?"

"Of course, father. Before, I had no idea of the hardships we were going through, but now I do. Don't worry about it anymore. Today I'll board that ship and I'll be back in a few months."

Juan Romero looked at him and thought his wife was right, Simón was just a child who was about to be sent to distant lands with an uncertain future.

"That's the spirit, being brave. Come, give me a hug."

Simón hugged his father tightly and they stood like that for a moment. Then, his father said:

"When you say goodbye to your mother, don't you dare shed a tear. She's very sensitive about your departure. So, you know, be strong."

"I will, father. Don't worry about that."

"Come on, let's have breakfast, your mother has prepared an incredible breakfast for you. It's like the king is coming."

"Really?"

"Of course, come on, come on, the bread is getting cold."

They crossed the beach towards their house, accompanied by the sounds of the waves breaking on the shore and their footsteps on the stones of the Triana beach.

Simón Romero arrived at the ship at the scheduled time. He approached the gangway that connected to the boat and stopped. He looked at it carefully and thought that this shell would be his home for the next few months. He was nervous, his right leg wouldn't stop trembling, and he still had that strange sensation in the pit of his stomach, a weight that almost prevented him from breathing. He felt weird. It was the first time he was leaving his home and he had a sea of uncertainties in front of him. It was the first time he thought about the future, his future. From the moment he set foot on Las Ánimas' deck, a new world he knew nothing about would open up to him, leaving behind what had been his life until then.

He crossed the gangway and, with a jump, landed on the deck. The sailors on board glanced at him and continued with their work. One was cleaning the pots and another, part of the bow.

Benjamin, the boatswain, came to meet him and said:

"Welcome aboard, cabin boy."

"My name is Simón Romero."

"I'm Benjamin, the boatswain, the second in command. I'll show you where you'll sleep and the rules you need to follow."

"Alright, Mr. Boatswain."

"Follow me."

The cabin boy followed him into the ship. Upon entering, he noticed a very strong smell that was everywhere and made him cover his nose.

"It's the smell of fish, it comes from the holds. You'll get used to it. No matter how much we clean, the stench doesn't go away. When we clean the fish, the blood seeps through the cracks in the wood and gets everywhere. That's why one of the rules the captain has imposed is to wash every night before getting into bed. Later, I'll give you a piece of soap for your personal hygiene."

They reached the area where the dormitory was, which was a cubicle with more than twenty hammocks placed in parallel.

"Choose an empty one. Put your clothes on it and get up because you have tasks to do."

"Thank you."

The boatswain left and Simón was left alone in the compartment. The smell of fish had also seeped in there. It was a matter of getting used to it, he thought. He found an empty hammock in a corner. He shook it, put his clothes on it, and went up on deck.

There he found the boatswain with the rest of the sailors. When Simón joined the group, Benjamin said:

"Well, cabin boy, take that bucket and start cleaning from stern to bow."

"What's the stern and the bow?"

The boatswain smiled and said:

"This is the first lesson you'll learn, cabin boy."

"My name is Simón Romero Arráez, sir."

"For a few months, you'll be Mr. Cabin Boy to me, understood?"

"Yes, sir, and what does cabin boy mean?"

"You're quite the questioner... I like that. Cabin boy means apprentice sailor. The stern is that part— "he said, pointing to the back of the ship— "See that it's a bit wider than the front, which is called the bow. For you to understand, if you were a ship, your back would be the stern and your chest, the bow. In short, the bow is the front part of the ship and the stern, the back. We also have port and starboard, which are very important when we're sailing. If you face the bow, starboard is the right side of the ship and port is the left side. Do you understand, cabin boy?"

Simón said nothing. He stood on the deck with his face facing the front of the ship, raised his right hand, and said:

"Starboard."

Then he raised his left and said:

"Port."

"You learn fast, cabin boy. So start cleaning from stern to bow and don't forget the cracks on port and starboard. The filth loves to hide in them, so you have to work thoroughly."

The apprentice sailor took the bucket and brush and started cleaning the deck in the direction the boatswain had told him while memorizing the terms he had learned by repeating them to himself in a low voice.

In the afternoon, he was assigned new cleaning tasks and ended up exhausted, so much so that he didn't

feel like eating dinner. After the boatswain authorized him, he went down to the compartment where the hammocks were, found his own, and lay down. He reviewed the terms he had learned. He fell asleep thinking about them, aided by the gentle rocking of the boat, which moved from stern to bow and from starboard to port.

A loud shout woke him up.

"Cabin boy, it's time to get up! I think you've slept enough and it's time for breakfast," the boatswain said.

Simón got up, he had rested well. The only thing he remembered from the night before were the blisters on both hands, but he knew they would soon harden, that it was just a matter of time and hard work.

A faint smell of hot food indicated the way he had to go. At that moment, he was hungry. Not having eaten anything during the night made his stomach sing incessantly. He crossed the narrow hallway until he reached a room where the sailors were enjoying breakfast.

The boatswain said to him:

"Here's a place for you to sit. Take advantage because today there's hot milk. It will be the last you drink for many months. Also, eat bread, there's still some left, and some cheese. This is the only fresh food you'll see for some time. Fresh food will be a luxury when we're a week at sea. Take advantage of this opportunity. When you finish, go up on deck without delay. We're waiting for you."

"Thank you, sir."

The young cabin boy sat down, served himself some milk in a wooden bowl, took a piece of cheese, a good piece of bread, and began to eat.

He remembered the breakfast his mother had prepared for him the morning before. Now, that was a proper breakfast. He was going to miss his mother's cooking; he was really going to miss it.

The sailors with him finished eating. He was left alone and, when he finished, he went up on deck.

Captain Juan Sánchez was in the center of the ship surrounded by the sailors who made up his crew. He glanced one by one at each of his men, those who were going to accompany him to seek sustenance for several months.

Most of them were boys who were not yet twenty years old, and five of them had no experience at sea. They would have to learn quickly and adapt to the harsh conditions of working on a fishing boat.

The captain knew that he was increasingly having difficulty finding experienced men willing to enlist to go to Africa. The fear of pirates was a contagious virus spreading among the sailors of Las Palmas. However, there was no shortage of boys willing to take the risk because it was the only way to bring some money home.

The Canary Islands had become, after their conquest by the Crown of Castile in the fifteenth century and the subsequent discovery of America, a strategic point for the development of Spain as a world power. The Canary Islands, especially Gran Canaria and Tenerife, were an obligatory stopping point for ships going to or coming from the New World. This fact did not go unnoticed by French, Dutch, English, and Berber pirates and privateers who lurked and attacked ships following this route.

The captain took a step forward and addressed them:

"Before the sun rises on the horizon, we will be on our way to Berbería. I know many of you are afraid of the possibility of being attacked and, as a consequence, being sold as slaves to the Moors of Algiers. That's a risk we have to take. A risk that will be paid at a good price, I assure you. At the end of the fishing season, I will pay you, but keep in mind that your salary will depend on the fish we're able to catch. So you have to work very hard if you want to take home some coins for your families. Don't forget, work, work, and then work. Breakfast, lunch, and dinner will depend on fishing, although normally we'll have breakfast at sunrise, lunch at noon, and dinner at nightfall. Remember, you have to eat well, food will never be lacking. From experience, I know that an underfed sailor doesn't perform, and I want you to perform to the best of your abilities. You know you'll be rewarded. Never forget that we're here to fish and it's hard work. Anyone who wants to can leave, but once we cast off, there's no turning back. Everyone take your place, we're setting off without delay."

He began to give the necessary orders to weigh anchor, release the ropes from the bow and stern, and unfurl the sails of the brigantine to set course for the coasts of Cape Bojador.

Simón didn't know where to go until he heard the boatswain's shout:

"Cabin boy! Go to the stern and grab the starboard line tightly."

Simón remembered what he had learned. So he went to the stern and started to gather the line that kept the ship moored to the shelter of the solid rock of the Las Palmas dock that a worker had released. When he finished gathering it, he saw his parents, who had come to bid him farewell.

"We'll be waiting for you, son! Come back soon!" his father shouted.

"Yes, father, I'll come back, I promise."

His mother stayed silent, wiping away tears, trying to control the anxiety that ran through her body, making her chest rise and fall like a boat in a storm.

Simón stayed in the same spot watching as, for the first time, he left behind what had been his life without knowing if he would fulfill the promise he had made to his father.

He headed towards the bow. He felt the sea breeze caress his face and realized that the trade wind was blowing vigorously, inflating the two lateen sails of the brigantine, propelling it towards distant and unknown horizons.

The apprenticeship

Out on the high seas, three young boys were huddled on the starboard side, retching due to the incessant rocking from bow to stern, from starboard to port, and back again. When they had nearly recovered, the captain called them over.

"I see you're struggling a bit, but that's normal," he said. "We've all been through it. In a few days, you'll be fine. It's just a matter of time and adaptation. If anyone is still vomiting after three days, don't worry, we'll throw them overboard to be shark bait. Then I'll give you a concoction that'll work wonders for seasickness," he added with a sly grin.

The three boys paled, imagining what the captain had just told them.

"But the sharks can wait a few days. I need a volunteer to climb up the mainmast and release the sail, which isn't catching as well as it should. Anyone brave enough?" he asked, addressing them.

Simón stepped forward. "What do I need to do, sir?"

"You need to climb up this mast," the captain said, patting the mainmast. "See that wrinkle there? You need to reach it, pull the sail, and release it."

"Understood," Simón responded determinedly.

Without hesitation, he climbed like a monkey until he reached the spot indicated by his captain. He maneuvered skillfully to avoid falling and swiftly resolved the issue. As he descended, the mate said to him, "Like you've been doing it your whole life. I think we have a future good sailor here."

He wasn't wrong.

Six days into their voyage, with the wind in their favor and the sea calm, they reached Cape Bojador at dawn. Dropping anchor, they moored half a mile from three fishing vessels hard at work. The captain called them to the deck again.

"There's good fishing, so let's not waste time. First, we'll gather enough bait; then, grab the rods and lines and start fishing."

Within an hour and a half, they had enough bait to start. Simón and the boys watched eagerly as their companions went to work until the boatswain shouted at them.

"What are you standing around for? Grab a rod and start fishing. You learn by doing."

Simón was the first to get to work. He took a rod, watched the companion beside him, and imitated his movements. From one of the wooden barrels, he hooked a lively six-centimeter-long fry, cast it into the sea, and soon shouted with enthusiasm, "I've got one, I've got one!"

"Pull the rod tight so it doesn't escape. Keep it firm and give it a strong, sharp tug toward the deck," the sailor beside him instructed.

He followed the experienced fisherman's instructions, keeping the rod firm, giving a tug, and watching an splendid snapper rise to the deck. With a quick motion, he removed the hook from the fish's mouth, took bait, placed it on the hook, and cast it into the sea. Cast after cast, he became skilled with the rod, his movements becoming faster and more precise.

A few hours before nightfall, the captain said, "That's enough for today. There's no room left on deck for another fish. It's been a fruitful day. We need to get started on salting them without wasting time."

The fishermen gathered on deck. With razor-sharp machetes, they cut off the fish's heads, split them open, removed the backbone, salted them, and stacked them in wooden crates. They continued until night fell.

The young fisherman finished his first day exhausted. His hands, shoulders, and waist ached. He felt like his kidneys were about to burst from pain. He sat down at the table to eat. He devoured the plate of lentils and the five flour biscuits they had given him, washed down with a bit of fresh water.

Dragging his feet, he headed to his hammock and lay down. He closed his eyes, but he couldn't sleep. Fatigue and pain prevented it. He saw someone approaching with a lantern, stopping at each bunk. He heard murmurs but couldn't distinguish who it was or what they were saying until they reached his hammock. It was the captain.

"You did a good job today, deckhand. You worked hard and without stopping. You'll be a great fisherman and a great sailor. Here, drink this concoction. It'll ease the pain and help you sleep," the captain said.

"What is it?"

"It's a mixture of poppy extract, lemon balm, chamomile, ginger, lemon verbena, and a little rum with honey."

Simón took a sip and liked it, so he took another, and then another. He needed something to ease the pain.

"Easy, sailor! Three sips will do the trick," the captain said, taking the bottle from him.

The boy felt the rum's effects in his throat, as it went down his esophagus and warmed his stomach.

"Let's see those hands; I'm sure they're full of blisters," the captain said.

He took the boy's hands and brought the oil lamp closer. He found some blisters on the fingers.

"I thought they'd be in worse condition."

"The boatswain gave me two pieces of cloth to wrap around my hands, so I did. It would be more comfortable for me to fish that way."

"Little by little, calluses will form, and you won't need any cloth, but until then, rub this plant on your hands, face, and neck. It's aloe; it'll ease the pain and heal your blisters and sunburns. There are five aloe plants in the stern. Use it for any wounds you get. Apply it every day. It's miraculous. Ask the cook to show you how to cut it."

Simón took the piece of aloe. It felt cool like water and slightly sticky. He rubbed it on his hands, then his forearms, and finished with his neck. He felt coolness and relief where he'd applied the miraculous plant.

The drink took effect, and he fell asleep like a log.

Before dawn, they were back at work, starting to fish again. They continued like this for many days, resting only to eat and to salt their catch. As the captain had said, the mission was to catch thirty thousand fish, and once achieved, they would return home.

After twenty-six days of uninterrupted fishing, they had almost reached their goal. Juan Sánchez called them over just past noon and informed them, "We've done an excellent job. We have enough to go back and make a good profit, so after lunch, we'll weigh anchor and head home."

The sailors, without exception, jumped for joy at the news. They were eager to return to their homes.

At noon, they weighed anchor and set sail for Gran Canaria. Three days of sailing close-hauled and a night of battling a strong swell later, the calm set in. They spent a whole day with no wind blowing. As night fell, a light breeze began to rise from the northwest, and by midnight, it had become a strong, steady wind that filled the sails to continue their course towards the Canary shores.

At dawn on the sixth day, a piercing cry echoed through the ship:

"Pirates! Pirates! To port!" shouted the boatswain.

"To your stations, reef the mainsail more!" the captain yelled, changing course at the same time.

The pirate ship was closing in fast due to its greater speed and better maneuverability. The captain tried to escape the attack, but they could do little against the power and speed of the Berber corsair ship. Furthermore, the thousands of kilos in the hold of the fishing vessel hindered their escape maneuvers.

The fishing boat zigzagged for several miles, but with each turn of the brigantine, the corsairs responded with a much faster turn, closing in inexorably. In one of these escape maneuvers, the brigantine was boarded on the starboard side. Before they realized it, thirty-five corsairs were on the deck of the fishing vessel, their weapons ready for battle.

The captain, fearing that some brave sailor might use the salted fish machete to repel the attack, shouted, "Stop! There's nothing to be done. They outnumber us. They won't hesitate to slit our throats."

After a few minutes of commotion, of some blows and shoving, the captain of the corsairs boarded. He walked slowly across the deck until he reached the stern of the ship and, grabbing the helm, asked in perfect Spanish, though with a rolling "r":

"Who is the captain?"

Juan Sánchez stepped forward and said, with a very serious face, "I am."

The Master knew that his life as a fisherman had ended, and so had those of his crew. The worst omens had come true. He knew that their fate would be nothing other than being sold as slaves in some market on the African coast.

"You're a prudent and intelligent man because you've avoided bloodshed. It's a detail that speaks volumes about you. You're also a good sailor. It took me a long time to catch up to your ship. It's been a while since a fishing boat has put up so much resistance to being captured. It was only a matter of time. But let's get to the important part. What do you have in your hold?"

"Twenty-eight thousand pieces of salted fish," replied the captain, knowing that all their hard work would be in vain.

"You've done well in this catch, it seems."

"Hard work pays off, a fruitless endeavor, it seems."

"You're not wrong. Do you know who I am?" asked the Berber.

"No, I haven't had that pleasure. This is the first time I've encountered a corsair, despite many years of sailing and fishing these seas."

"They call me El Kaid, sir and corsair, although many people question the 'sir' part. As you can imagine, we'll take your ship and cargo, and you will be sold as slaves in Algiers."

Upon hearing this, there was a small commotion among the sailors. Simón thought that his worst nightmares had finally come true, those where he saw himself chained and sold as a miserable slave. However, in an unexpected leap, he snatched the saber from the Berber next to him, placed it at his throat, and shouted at El Kaid:

"It won't be so easy to capture me, devilish Moor!"

"We've got a brave sailor here. Cut his throat if you wish," El Kaid said coldly. "You'll be the next to serve as shark bait. Courage at sea is important, but recklessness and temerity can lead to death, young man."

"Simón, stop these antics and hand over the damn saber!" the captain shouted.

"You have a quite judicious captain, it seems. You only have one life; that's the main rule a sailor has to learn, and today is a good day to do so," the corsair said, smiling and disregarding the situation.

The young man pondered the situation. He knew that if he ended the bandit's life, they would end his without hesitation. Even if he dropped the weapon, that action would cost him his life. Tension filled the deck of the fishing vessel, and Juan Sánchez intervened again:

"Simón, listen to me. It's not worth it. You're a young and strong lad, and you'll get through this even as a slave. Your life is the most important."

"Your boss is a judicious man. I have no doubt," Simón said.

"Simón, please..." the captain pleaded once more.

Simón released the corsair and moved away from him. He kept the saber in his hand until finally throwing it to the ground and pushing it away with a slight kick of his left leg. The corsair picked up the saber, grabbed the young man, lifted him with the intention of attacking him, but El Kaid shouted:

"Put down that saber and your damned intention, or have you forgotten that he has a price? If you want to end his life, do it, but it will cost you. Nobody gives anything for free. If you want, take his life, but you'll have to pay me his value in gold, and you know that young men are highly valued in the slave markets. Don't forget that if you can't pay me, you'll pay with your life, which is the only valuable thing you have."

The corsair removed the fine steel of his sword from the young sailor's neck, sheathed it in the sash tied around his trousers, and pushed him away with a strong shove that made Simón roll across the deck.

"Now that the storm has passed and calm returns," he said mockingly, "let's set course for Algiers; we have a good deal on our hands. Take them to the hold of our ship and chain them. Leave the young rebel on deck. Hussein, choose some men to help you bring the fishing boat to a safe harbor, and don't forget to make a list of the sailors we've captured."

They set course for the port of Algiers. On deck, Simón waited for El Kaid to arrive. The young man's face was serious, and fear was reflected in his expression. He did not know why he was not accompanying the sailors who had been his companions.

The corsair approached with firm steps, and when he stood in front of Simón, he said:

"I'm considering whether to sell you as a slave; I'm sure they would give me your weight in gold because you are a strong and healthy lad. Or to keep you in my service because you have qualities to be a good corsair. You're determined, brave, and audacious, three qualities that are very important for a corsair."

Children and adolescents were highly valued by corsairs because they could be easily convinced and would eventually not hesitate to convert to Islam and become the most faithful sailors.

Simón said nothing. He was considering whether to throw himself overboard and end it all or let fate guide him. Anger and helplessness boiled in his head. He cursed his bad luck, which translated into being captured by the Moors on his first voyage. He looked toward the horizon, where he thought his land was, a land he did not know if he would ever set foot on again. His fishing adventure had ended suddenly, as if lightning had struck it. However, Simón was a pragmatic lad and knew he had no choice but to adapt and acquiesce.

"What do you want? Because I see you have some determination. Few men have the courage to face me and live. Those who have dared are at the bottom of the sea. In a way, I have to admit that I find you sympathetic."

"I don't care what you do with my life. If you want to sell me, do it; if you want to throw me to the sharks, you can do that too. I'll accept my fate as a good Christian."

"Oh, as a good Christian. Well, let's do this. You'll stay with me for a while. If during that time you turn out to be what I think you are, you'll stay in my service, and if not, I'll sell you to the highest bidder. What do you say?"

"I've already said I'll accept my fate."

And so El Kaid resolved the matter. He had a good eye for assessing people's abilities, and most of his pirates were slaves who had become his crew and corsairs over time.

The corsair ship arrived in Algiers. Simón was amazed as he entered the bustling port, which had nothing to do with the pier of Las Palmas. This one was filled with ships coming and going through its mouth. He had never seen anything like it. The sight was impressive.

The corsair vessel entered the innermost part of the port and docked at the pier facing the city's entrance.

Simón watched as his former companions emerged in chains and were put into a cart. He looked at El Kaid

, disembarked from the ship, and slowly made his way toward the cart. He searched for the captain, found him sitting in the back with a lost look.

"Captain! Captain!" called Simón.

The captain turned his head toward the young man as if awakening from a dream. He looked at him, smiled, and said:

"Simón, remember that the most important thing is to preserve life. In a way, you've been very lucky because you could be here with us. That corsair seems like a sensible man. Don't squander the opportunity. You're a strong, intelligent, and very brave lad."

"Thank you, Captain. I hope I'll be lucky."

"I hope so too, Simón."

The cart set off, and Simón watched it disappear through the city's streets. He stood still amidst the bustle of the port, not hearing the shouts of the sailors, nor the cries and lamentations of the captives, nor the flutter of the sails, nor the song of the seagulls. He thought he should be with them and that this had to be his destiny. He thought of running toward the sea and jumping like the stones he threw on the beach of Triana, jumping and jumping until he exhausted himself to escape from this situation he had never imagined even in his dreams. However, he was not a stone; he was a captive, a slave.

A voice snapped him out of his stupor. He turned and saw the figure of El Kaid.

"Never forget that you are the master of your own destiny, lad. When luck passes by your house, you just have to reach out, grab it, and not let it slip away. Being a slave is not a pleasant experience. Think that you've been lucky. A lad like you would fetch a good price at the market, and with luck, you could end up as a handsome young slave serving a wealthy merchant, or conversely, end up rowing to exhaustion in a galley."

"Why do you capture ships and sell slaves?"

"Because I don't know how to do anything else, Simón," he called him by his name for the first time. "Life gives you opportunities, and you have two options: seize them or let them go. This is a good business.

It has its dangers, but it pays well. I'm a fisherman who catches ships and slaves. You may like it or not, but this is what we do."

"The people in that cart are my countrymen. The master treated me well and gave me the opportunity to earn a living. What will happen to them?"

"Tomorrow at noon, they will be sold in a plaza near the Palace of Jenina, better known as the Baths of Algiers. Those who are lucky will go as slaves to the mansions of the lords of this city, especially the youngest ones; those who are not, will go to the galleys."

"If I had money, I would buy their freedom."

"To do that, first, you'll have to be a free man and buy your own freedom, and second, you'll have to gather a lot of money. I told you the other day, I give you the opportunity to join my crew; if you don't want to, I'll sell you as a slave."

The lad knew he had no other choice but to accept the corsair's offer. A future as a slave in Algiers was not very promising. He had no option.

"I'll join your crew and hope to buy my freedom someday," he said determinedly.

"I think I haven't been mistaken about you, but everything has a price, sailor, and from the moment we sail out of that port, you'll be paying for your freedom. Most of my men are free, and most were slaves."

"Why didn't you sell me as a slave?"

The corsair smiled and said, "For two reasons. First, I think you'll be a good sailor and a good corsair, and second, you resemble my son Ali very much. He was a very special boy, and you have the same sparkle in your eyes. Ali didn't live to see his fifteenth birthday. Infected pustules invaded his body and consumed him in less than a month. You remind me a lot of him. Brave, impetuous, and strong."

Simón thought that parents should never bury their children. It was a very sad story, and he felt sorry for the corsair.

"But I'm not your son, sir, and I never will be. I'm Simón Romero Arráez."

"I know you'll never be, and I'm not looking for a replacement, but I like seeing a young lad wandering around my ship as he did. I have ten children, six girls and four boys. Ali was the only one determined to follow in my footsteps. He also wanted to be a corsair. He learned very quickly, always asking about what he didn't know. He was a true sponge of the sea. So now you know the real reason why I haven't sold you. It's up to you to become a good sailor and then a good corsair to buy your freedom in a few years."

Simón listened to El Kaid's words.

"In three days," the corsair continued, "we'll set sail again. I've arranged for them to find you a place to sleep on board. Don't try to escape, Simón. Algiers is a very dangerous place for a lad your age. This is the only place where you'll be safe. Convince yourself; this ship will be your home for the next few years."

"Don't worry; I won't escape. I'll be here."

Simón boarded the ship accompanied by El Kaid, who showed him to his quarters: a small corner with a hammock blackened by use.

"You'll be fine here. Keep it clean, and you'll sleep better. Don't forget to wash yourself every day. At noon, come up for meals. We have a good cook on board. When we're docked in port, the meals are sumptuous and very appetizing, made with fresh produce. Don't miss them. You need to eat to stay strong and avoid diseases."

"Thank you, sir."

"Rest as much as you can. We'll set sail in two days."

Simón watched as the corsair left the quarters. He opened the hammock and lay down. He looked up at the ceiling, which was three handspans from his face. It smelled of damp, but not of fish, and he smiled for the first time in many days. At least, he wouldn't smell like fish anymore.

He closed his eyes and tried to sleep. He breathed deeply and thought of his parents and whether they would ever find out that he had been made a slave. He would find a way to let them know, to tell them he was fine and not to worry.

He focused on his breathing and the rocking of the ship and fell asleep. He dreamed of playing on his beach in Triana, throwing stones and making them fly over the waves, and then going fishing with his brother Gaspar. They caught a shark bigger than their skiff, and Captain Juan Sánchez helped them hoist it onto the boat. Dreams are like that; we're not their owners.

The first approach

Three days later, they set sail for the shores of Barbary. El Kaid's ship was a two-masted xebec with two immense lateen sails that allowed it to sail perfectly close-hauled and gave it a manifest superiority on this course. El Kaid knew this and forced this direction to end up hunting his rivals. The vessel was equipped for attack and boarding. A war machine in every sense. The corsair had reinforced the bow with metal pieces to give it greater resistance in boarding actions.

They sailed for more than ten days during which Simón performed maintenance tasks, such as cleaning the deck, helping in the kitchen, cleaning the latrines at the bow and stern, acting as a lookout, and collaborating in navigation maneuvers, especially in tacks where many hands were needed.

Simón quickly learned the concepts of navigation and never stopped asking how to handle a ship, how to tack, and how to maintain course.

El Kaid watched him closely and was certain that he would soon become a great sailor because he not only had the necessary attitude but also had plenty of qualities to be one.

On the ninth day of sailing, as dusk was approaching, the corsair called him and took him to the stern. He moved aside the sailor in charge of steering the ship, took the helm, and said, "You're working very hard, Simón. I'm proud of you. My men are beginning to respect you. It's clear as day that you're eager to learn. You're a very ambitious lad."

"I like what I do, sir. What else can I do here but work and learn? I don't want to be idle."

"I know. Many of my men are lazy and need to be prodded to do their tasks. Not you. You're willing to work, and I like that very much."

"I tell you, sir, time flies when I'm busy. Before I know it, night has fallen, and all I have left is to rest to start the next day with enthusiasm."

"Do you want to take the helm?" the corsair asked with a smile.

Simón looked up at the lateen sails carrying the ship towards its course. He felt the force of the ship, which almost flew over the sea like a seagull, as if it had a life of its own.

"Yes, I would like to try," he replied with a half-smile.

"It's not easy, sailor. You have to keep the tiller centered to maintain the course. Steer it with your hands, whisper in its ear that you're the one in charge, and take it where you want it to go."

"I'm not sure if I can, sir," he said fearfully.

"I know you can. I'll be by your side, Simón. Take it."

El Kaid stepped aside and left the tiller unattended for a moment. Simón took it. His heart began to beat strongly, and his hands started to sweat. There he understood the corsair's words. The ship seemed to have a life of its own, and the tiller pulled strongly to starboard. Simón pulled it forcefully towards the center, and the ship responded.

"What do you feel?" the corsair asked with great interest.

"It pulls a lot to starboard, as if it wanted to go in that direction. It seems alive and wants to go where it wants."

"Well, you have to be there to tell it that you set the course. We're in its hands, sailor."

He stayed like that for a few minutes until night fell completely. The sailors began to light the lanterns on the deck, allowing them to move about somewhat freely to avoid tripping and falling overboard.

"I can't see anything, sir. How do we navigate at night without getting lost in the vastness of the ocean?"

"Look at the sky. Do you see the stars?"

Simón looked up and saw a myriad of stars twinkling in the darkness. It wasn't the first time he had stopped to contemplate the sky at night. He had done it many times at his home in Las Palmas, on warm summer nights, when the dry winds from the south blew. He would go down to Triana Beach, lie down on the pebbles, and lose himself in the immensity of the universe, counting the number of shooting stars that crossed the sky.

"Yes, they're beautiful. Many times I wonder what's up there."

"They're the ones that guide us at night. Their position in the sky allows us to know the almost exact course we're on, and so it's very difficult to get lost. However, you need experience and a lot of knowledge not to get lost in the vastness of the ocean. I think for today, it's more than enough, sailor. We'll leave the helm to Mohamed; he'll take us to our destination."

"Where are we going, sir?" Simón asked as he handed the tiller to the sailor.

"Toward the British coast. If we're lucky, we can capture a great ship and rest for a few months. But we're taking a big risk. They usually have very good ships and are protected by many cannons that would shred us in a direct confrontation. So we have to be very cautious and know who we're attacking. Never forget that a timely retreat is also a victory. Corsairs have to learn to flee when necessary."

"Thank you, sir. I've loved steering your ship."

"You'll gain more experience, and one day you'll be able to sail it alone and even have and sail your own ship. It's time for you to go to sleep, Simón."

Simón Romero crossed the deck, descended, and went to his corner. With a leap, he climbed into his hammock and thought about the words El Kaid had said to him: "One day you'll be able to sail it alone and even have and sail your own ship." "My own ship," he thought. From then on, he set out to achieve that dream and visualized himself on his own ship, crossing the seas and pursuing his dreams.

***

At dawn, he was awakened by a sailor's cry:

"Ship in sight! Ship in sight! Ship in sight!"

Simón got up as quickly as he could, went up on deck, and found the corsair, who was speaking with his crew.

El Kaid ordered the pirates to gather on deck and addressed them in a solemn tone:

"Be alert to my orders. We'll only attack if the ship is within our reach. Mohamed," he indicated to the helmsman, "point the bow in the direction of that ship and take us to it without delay. Maintain course and be attentive to my words."

El Kaid took a spyglass and directed it towards the vessel on the starboard side. He observed that it had three masts and flew the Portuguese flag on the mainmast. Then he directed the lenses towards the deck, searching for any traces of cannons. He counted six, two at the bow, two on the starboard side, and two on the port side. The corsair knew what that meant. It was a merchant ship returning from the Americas. They had stumbled upon a diamond lost in the ocean.

"We've been fortunate. I believe it's a Portuguese merchant galleon possibly coming from America. Be prepared to initiate boarding. You know the rules: minimal casualties and minimal damage to the ship. Mohamed, steer the bow towards it."

Simón stood paralyzed, unsure of what to do. He found himself in the center of the deck alone while the rest of the crew was at their stations, confident in what to do when the opportune moment arrived. He heard El Kaid calling him:

"Simón, come here!"

Simón ran to his side.

"Tell me, sir. I don't know what to do. I'm lost," he said, stumbling over his words.

"Don't worry, lad. We're going to see what you're made of, sailor. Take this dagger," he said, handing him a double-edged dagger so shiny that the young man's face reflected like a mirror, topped with a white ivory handle.

"I'll do as you order, sir," he replied with a mix of nervousness and excitement.

"When we board the Portuguese merchant, I want you to jump and climb the mainmast, as high as you can, and slash both sails from top to bottom. Stick the dagger in the center of the sail, near the mainmast, your weight will do the rest. Drive the blade in up to the hilt and keep the dagger pressed against the sail so you don't fall into the void. Do you understand?"

"Is the mainmast the one in the center of the ship?"

"Exactly, Simón. That will be your mission. Be very careful and go straight to the mast. Don't stop for anything or anyone. Run as if your life depended on it. Climb the mast as fast as you can. I'm sure you'll do fine. And don't forget to drive the blade in all the way."

"I'll try to do my best, sir," said Simón with determination.

The merchant ship veered round when it noticed the presence of the corsair vessel and, at the same time, fired the first cannon shot.

El Kaid ordered the helmsman to veer. The sailors performed the maneuver as one, as if they were a single man, and the xebec responded quickly.

The merchant ship continued firing its cannons without managing to hit the corsair ship. Hitting a moving target was nearly impossible, especially a vessel as swift as El Kaid's xebec.

When the experienced corsair knew the merchant was within range, he instructed the helmsman to position themselves aft to avoid the enemy's cannon fire.

When they were just a few meters away, El Kaid ordered the helmsman to position themselves to windward and, when they were in this favorable position, he shouted:

"Ready for boarding!"

The corsair ship positioned itself a few meters from the Portuguese ship's port side, and the two ships collided. A deafening sound rang out from the scraping of the two hulls, and the boarding commenced.

The corsair seized Simón by the shoulders, looked him in the eyes, and said:

"Simón, it's your turn. Good luck, lad, and be very careful."

"Thank you, sir," Simón said, jumping onto the boarded ship.

He ran across the deck with the dagger in his sash, dodging his comrades and enemies alike. Upon reaching the center of the ship, he leaped onto one of the ropes of the galleon's shrouds and propelled himself up. He grabbed hold of the ropes of two shrouds and climbed like a cat to the top of the mast. He positioned himself in the center, drew the dagger from his waist, plunged it into the sail up to the hilt, and let himself fall. The sail tore as if it were paper. Upon reaching the second sail, Simón grabbed the first rope he found, buried the dagger in the fabric again, and let himself fall until it split in two.

Then, he tucked the knife into his sash, jumped onto the deck, and ran to the bow mast. He climbed up the shroud ropes, repeated the same maneuver, and slashed the two sails.

The merchant ship lost speed like a wounded and tired animal until it finally stopped. Simón ran across the deck and returned to where El Kaid was standing, who smiled upon seeing him and said:

"Good work, lad. Fast, efficient, and with initiative. I saw that you made the decision to slash the sails at the bow. That was another sailor's mission, but he must have fallen in battle. You completed the task excellently."

After several minutes, only the flapping of the galleon's square sails and the lateen sails of the xebec could be heard.

El Kaid jumped onto the Portuguese ship and inquired about the captain.

Two of his crew members had the captain and brought him to the corsair, who stepped forward and said:

"I am El Kaid. Your ship and its contents are now in the hands of Algiers. What do you have in your holds?"

The captain remained silent until one of the corsairs put his saber to his throat and told him to answer.

"A cargo of gold, silver, and precious stones for Juan IV of Portugal."

"Gold, silver, and precious stones. We've found a treasure floating on the sea."

"We beg you to take what you deem fit and then let us continue on our way."

"Haha, a good try, my friend! This ship is worth its weight in gold, and so is its crew. You know that everything is fair game at sea. You will descend to the hold and stay there until we reach the port of Algiers. Don't worry, you won't lack water or food. Corsairs have a bad reputation. Some compare us to the devil himself of the Christians. Your sailors will be under our orders. Designate a group of four to take care of your provisions and another eight to repair the sails. You, captain, make a list with the names, surnames, age, gender, position, and noble title, if any, of your crew. Don't leave anyone out, and don't try to deceive me. In the end, we always find out who's who."

"Perhaps we could reach an agreement, a compromise on my part to send you the amount you deem fit for the value of our persons."

The corsair walked from port to starboard, weighing the captain's words.

"You're a good negotiator, there's no doubt about that, but that would be a bad deal, and you know it. Let's not waste any more time on nonsense that will get us nowhere. You have work to do, so get to it."

El Kaid ordered ten of his men to oversee the transfer of the captives to the holds of the ship. Once the sails were repaired, they would set sail.

Simón followed his leader back to the corsair ship, and once there, El Kaid commented:

"We rarely encounter a ship like this, and if we do, it's usually escorted by a heavily armed ship with twenty guns per side. The sea is so vast that many risk crossing the Atlantic without proper protection. It's like finding a needle in a haystack, as the Spanish saying goes."

Simón thought about the last comment and realized it was true. In the days they had been sailing, they hadn't encountered any other ships, only dolphins and whales.

"Why didn't you use the cannon on the starboard side to try to stop the ship? It would have been easier."

"Yes, we would have stopped it faster by splitting the masts in two, riddling the hull with holes, and leaving it half-sunk. We would have had enough time to capture the captives and the treasure they carry on board. But, there's always a 'but,' Simón; a corsair knows the value of a ship in good condition, especially a merchant like this one. For that reason, we try to cause the least damage possible, even if it takes us longer to capture it. Objectives are achieved with time and tenacity. Never forget that, sailor. Also, that cannon we only use for defense, and many times I've thought about throwing it overboard or selling it. It's a burden that hampers our maneuvers. Corsair ships need to be light and fast because our success depends on those two characteristics. If you ever have a ship, never put cannons on it."

"What will we do?"

"Return to Algiers, Simón. We'll rest for a few months and then we'll set sail again. That's our fate. Arrive and set sail again. What do you think?"

"I think it's good, sir. Very good."

Simón Romero stayed on the deck, awestruck by the majesty of the captured ship. He felt satisfied. He had performed the task assigned to him by El Kaid very well, and his action had been decisive in successfully concluding the boarding.

***

Simón earned the respect of the corsairs, but above all, that of El Kaid, who saw in him the person who could become his right-hand man over time. Under the old corsair's orders, he began to assume new leadership responsibilities, and over time, he became the second in command. El Kaid knew he could trust him not only for his loyalty but also for the maritime knowledge he acquired rapidly in just a few years. Thus, the corsair entrusted him with matters related to boarding because he knew the Canary Islander was very skilled and would never let him down.

In this way, Simón Romero became a great Berber pirate admired by friend and foe alike, and El Kaid felt satisfied, very satisfied.

The Islam

Well into the year 1659, as they entered the port of Algiers, Simón wanted to speak with El Kaid. He climbed up to the deck where the Algerian corsair was and said:

"I've been sailing these seas for four years. You've given me the opportunity to earn enough to buy my freedom, and I believe I deserve it. Besides, I want to convert to Islam. After what I've seen, I no longer want to be a Christian. I like the corsair life, and I don't think I'll ever return to my homeland."

"It's true that you've been a faithful sailor. In these four years, you've worked hard in all the tasks I've assigned you, and I believe you deserve freedom. When we disembark, we'll go to the Great Mosque of Algiers, and your wishes will be fulfilled."

"Thank you. One last thing, sir. I would like to continue sailing by your side after I become a free man."

"I expected nothing less from you. In this time, you've proven your worth as a corsair, and having you by my side is a guarantee. You're the best man I've had under my command in a long time. I know that one day you'll leave this nest, and if you don't, I'll kick you out to find your own ship and be your own boss."

Simón knew that sooner or later he would do it; it was just a matter of time. But he was also aware that he still had much to learn, and the old corsair was a true master. He would be by his side until he completed his training or until the corsair kicked him out, as he had said.

"I'm in no hurry, sir. I'm very comfortable here, and every day I learn something new. If I'm a good corsair, it's thanks to you."

"From today on, don't call me sir, call me El Kaid. You're no longer a slave; you're a free man."

"It will be very difficult for me not to call you sir. To me, you're still a sir, the person who has taught me what I know, and I'm very grateful to you."

"Try to remember. Let's go to the mosque; we need to speak with the imam."

They disembarked from the ship and headed to the Great Mosque of Djemmá el Kebir. They took off their shoes and entered the temple. Simón was amazed by the majesty of the religious building and the overwhelming silence that enveloped it, only broken by the litany of the prayers of the faithful.

Simón asked:

"What do I have to do to convert to Islam?"

"You have to testify to your faith through the shahāda, in which you acknowledge Allah as the only god and Muhammad as his messenger and prophet, but the imam will tell us what to do. Wait here; I'll return with him," El Kaid told him.

Shortly afterward, the corsair arrived with an old man who walked very slowly. He had a whitish beard that reached his chest, a white robe that covered him from head to toe, and a tasbih in his right hand with beads of ivory darkened by use. He approached the young Canary Islander, observed him for a few moments, and then asked, dragging his words:

"Were you baptized in the religion of the prophet Jesus of Nazareth?"

"Yes, I was baptized at birth."

"Do you come to this mosque of your own free will and with an open heart to embrace the one God, Allah?"

"Yes, I come of my own free will, and for over two years, I have been practicing the Islamic religion."

"Then, my son, face towards Mecca and respond to my words. Do you acknowledge Allah as the only God and Muhammad as his prophet?"

"Yes, I acknowledge them."

"Do you acknowledge that Jesus of Nazareth is not the son of God but a prophet and subject of Allah?"

"Yes, I acknowledge it."

"With this act, you acknowledge that Islam is the true religion, that you are a slave to no one but Allah. You accept that what the prophet Muhammad says is revealed by Allah to enlighten our path to eternal happiness. In this act, you are born anew, and all your faults have been forgiven by the grace of Allah. You are clean of all blemish, pure as the crystalline water of a spring."

"Thank you, sir."

"As a new and pure man, you need a Muslim name. What would you like to be called?"

Simón didn't know what to answer, but he looked to El Kaid and asked him:

"What was your son's name, sir?"

El Kaid smiled, his eyes filled with tears of emotion, and replied:

"Ali, his name was Ali."

"I will call myself Ali Simón in honor of your son because, in a way, you are my father, sir."

"Thank you, Ali Simón. It's an honor for me that you bear my son's name."

"Ali Simón, servant of Allah, to complete your process, you must bathe with water to purify yourself. Never forget the five pillars of our religion: there is no other divinity than Allah, and Muhammad is his prophet, pray five times a day, give alms to the needy, fast during Ramadan, and pilgrimage to Mecca once in a lifetime if you can. You may go in peace, and may Allah guide you."

Ali Simón watched as the imam left as slowly as he had come, praying and moving the beads of his tasbih.

.

***

After the bath at the mosque, El Kaid and Ali Simon stopped at the exit. The corsair took him by the hand and said:

"Today you have made me very happy, Simon, Ali Simon. In a way, I didn't expect anything less from you. I lost a son for whom I mourned until my heart dried up, but I have gained another, and this event must be celebrated."

"It is an honor for me to bear your son's name."

"The honor is mine, Ali. I know you will make his name great because you are a man who will go far."

"Thank you, sir."

"A great celebration awaits us, befitting this great day."

After the Islamization celebration of Ali Simon Romero Arraez, they returned to the ship to set sail once again. El Kaid arrived after settling matters related to the slaves and merchandise in the holds. He boarded the ship and sought out the Canary. Finding him preparing the rigging to set sail, he called to him, and when he was by his side, he commented:

"Some captives from your land have arrived, Ali. One of your countrymen, also converted to Islam, is under the command of Mustafa Farid, a black corsair with a temper as foul as soot. He told me that if I was interested in buying any Canary Islanders because he knew they were good sailors. I took the list and read it. Among them, there was a name that caught my attention, an islander named Juan Romero, forty years old, and I thought he might be a relative of yours."

Ali Simon fell silent and said:

"By name and age, he could be my father, but he never thought of sailing to Barbary. I don't think it's him. So let's set sail, sir; we have a long way and much work ahead."

"Ali, the sea can wait, it's not going anywhere. If there's even a possibility that he's your father, we're going to check; if not, we'll leave when the tide rises. Is there such a possibility, son?"

"Yes, there is a possibility; he could be my father, but I don't want this issue to interfere with your business."

"My business is your business, Ali. Never forget that. If I win, you win; if I lose, you lose. We're in the same boat, so let's not speak more of it and let's go see if the captive is your father. Follow me."

Without wasting much time, they headed to the square north of the Palace of Jenina, which was the nerve center of the slave trade. They crossed narrow streets crowded with people heading to the city's different markets. After some inquiries, they found out where the Berber pirate named Mustafa Farid was. Ali Simon searched for his father among a crowd of captives of all races, mostly Central African blacks captured in the raids that pirates made on African coasts.

Ali Simon made his way through the crowd of buyers bidding on lots of slaves who were grouped and separated. He managed to position himself where he had a wide view of the square. He looked group by group until he managed to see him sitting, embracing his knees with his hands. He was thin and gaunt. He shouted his name:

"Juan Romero! Juan Romero!"

But the commotion in the square prevented his father from hearing his name, so he shouted again:

"Juan Romero! Juan Romero!"

Without thinking, he ran across the square. A soldier tried to stop him, but he pushed him aside. Another soldier, shouting, tried to block his path brandishing his saber. Then, Ali Simon drew his own and disarmed him with a swift stroke. His heart raced, and adrenaline ran through his veins like a rabid dog. The shouts died down, and the square fell silent. The onlookers were expectant to see what would happen. Soon after, he reached where his father was and shouted:

"Father, father!"

His father lifted his head slowly upon hearing his name and met his son's face. Emotion made him rise so quickly that he knocked over two captives who were next to him. For the first time in four long years, their gazes met again. They melted into a tight embrace, and his father said:

"Thank God you're alive, Simon! We knew you had been captured, but we lost track of you and heard nothing more. You've become a man, son. How big and strong you are!"

"Father, everything will be okay now. You're safe. Let's get out of here and talk calmly."

Simon looked at El Kaid and confirmed with a gesture that he was his father, while four guards surrounded them until the matter of the captive was resolved.

The old corsair crossed the square leisurely and approached where Mustafa was. They talked for a minute, and soon after, the issue of the ransom payment was resolved. One of the pirate's men crossed the human mass until he reached where Juan Romero and Ali Simon were and gestured that they could leave.

Juan Romero stopped. He looked at the group of Canarians waiting to be sold as slaves, who had witnessed the liberation of their comrade.

"What will happen to them, son?"

Ali Simon knew his father would never understand the sale of slaves no matter how much he explained it, and especially that he saw it as a normal and lawful activity, but that was the least of his worries.

"They will be sold, father. That is already known. Let's get out of here; there are many issues to resolve."

"Can't we do anything for them? They are our countrymen. Surely something can be done."

"No, father, we can't do anything. These are the rules of the game. We have to leave," Ali Simon told his father, taking him by the arm.

They crossed the square slowly and approached El Kaid. The Canarian introduced his father:

"Sir, this is my father, Juan Romero."

"It's a pleasure to meet the father of my best man: loyal, hardworking, and brave."

His father didn't know what to say to the man who wore a red turban, a white silk shirt, a black and blue silk vest, black harem pants, and a huge gray beard.

"Father, let me introduce you to El Kaid, my benefactor and protector during these years."

They shook hands firmly, and the corsair said:

"We need to delay our departure for as long as necessary, Ali. We will stay at my house until we solve the issue at hand. I imagine you want to return to your land as soon as possible."

"Yes, of course, that's the idea. My father will return to the Canaries on the first ship we find, sir," Ali Simon anticipated his father's response.

"No time to waste, Ali Simon. Let's go to my house. Your father will be taken care of properly and will be able to rest and recover."

Ali Simon had never been to El Kaid's house. He lived in a palace on the outskirts of the city built with limestone, giving it a pure appearance. At the entrance was a horseshoe arch, and inside, a large bright hall. On the sides were the rooms, whose entrances were topped with lobed arches.

El Kaid ordered his servants to attend to their guests, to prepare baths for them, and to start lunch. The servants led them to their rooms,

which were on the sides of the palace. After their respective baths, Ali Simon went to the room where his father was. He found him sitting in a white cotton robe with his hands on his face. His son asked him:

"What are you thinking about, father?"

"Why did he call you Ali?" he asked suddenly.

Ali Simon knew his father wouldn't like the answer, but he didn't want to lie to him, so he told him the truth.

"I converted to Islam today, father. From now on, my God is Allah, and Muhammad is his prophet. When I found out you were in Algiers, I was coming from the Great Mosque where I swore allegiance to Allah."

"But, son, you are a Christian. You were baptized, and that is a divine sacrament that cannot be broken so easily."

"No, father, I am not a Christian. I am a Muslim. When you baptized me, I couldn't choose. That sacrament was imposed on me. I didn't choose to be a Christian. Instead, I have chosen to be a Muslim freely. No one decided that for me."

Juan Romero did not understand what his son was saying. For him, taking him to the baptismal font was a great day, a day of joy and happiness. With the sacrament of baptism, evil was banished. His impure soul was transformed, by the grace of God, into a pure one, free from sin. Being a Christian was not up for discussion. It had been so since the beginning of time, and only infidels doubted that great truth.

"You know how they will call you. You will be called a renegade, a Moor, and an infidel, and I wouldn't like to hear one of my sons called that."

Ali Simon knew. Renegades were not well-regarded, and if they were captured, only the stake awaited them. He knew his Islamization was irreversible.

"I don't care what people say, father. My life is here, and so is my future. I have no intention of ever returning to the Canaries, father. I am a Muslim and a corsair."

"Son, are you going to raid ships and make slaves? Isn't there another way to make a living? A more Christian way?"

"Perhaps there is, but it's not in my plans. I am a corsair, and that's been my job since I was captured four years ago. I don't want or pretend to be anything else. I could have ended up rowing in a galley or serving a lord anywhere in the Mediterranean, but El Kaid gave me the opportunity to be a sailor and then a corsair. Today, I am a free man, although I am in debt to him. Your liberation has a price, but don't worry about that. We'll settle that matter in these days."

The Canarian knew that El Kaid had negotiated the payment with the Berber pirate, but he didn't know what that payment was, and that the pirate had accepted because the old corsair was well known and respected in the North African city.

"I know, son. I don't know how you're going to pay it. I don't even have a place to lay my head. I had to embark because I couldn't find work, and fishing in Barbary was the only option left to me even knowing that the Moors were on the coast. But when hunger strikes, you have to take a chance."

"And doesn't Salvador help you?"

"At first, yes. He started making some money as a shipwright, but more than two years ago, he got tired. He said that job wasn't for him. He joined a fishing boat, and I haven't heard from him. He said he wanted to become a pirate. We haven't heard from him since he left. So it's just your mother and me because your sisters got married, and the dowry we received for the marriages was a pittance. It gave us enough to survive for a year, but it ran out, I lost my job, and you know the rest of the story."

"Today we need to focus on arranging your departure to Gran Canaria. I will speak with El Kaid without fail to see how we can resolve it."

"Yes, I would like to go home as soon as possible, son. Your mother is alone, and I don't know how she's managing. I left her some money, but she won't have anything now. Thanks to your sisters, who, when I left, were delivering us a basket of vegetables and grains that solved our meals for a few days."

"Don't torment yourself, father. Mother will be fine; she is a strong and intelligent woman and will find a way to make a living. Besides, my sisters will take care of her. I have to go talk to El Kaid."

"Go in peace, son. I'll try to eat some of these delicacies they've put in our rooms, and then I want to rest a bit. I'm exhausted. My body weighs on me as if I were carrying an iron ball tied to my feet. I have to regain strength to go home."

"Eat and rest. We'll talk more later."

Ali Simon left his father in his room and went in search of the corsair. He crossed the main hall, asked one of the attendants, and was led to El Kaid's quarters. The servant entered, and he heard the Algerian's thunderous voice.

"Enter, Ali, you're at home!"

Ali entered and saw him lying on a large leather cushion drinking tea. He was accompanied by a young blonde with emerald green eyes who couldn't have been more than twenty years old and smiled as she also drank tea.

"Sit down, son. This is Maria, a beautiful Italian girl I captured over four years ago, who has remained in my service. Isn't she prettier than a sunrise?"

"It's true, sir."

"Don't call me sir. You're a free man. Just call me El Kaid. What do you want to talk to me about?"

"We'll have to rethink what we've discussed before because paying my father's ransom will leave me without resources to settle my freedom debt."

"I don't like changing plans, Ali. One of the things I admire in a man is generosity, especially if that generosity is with family. That's why I know you'll be a good Muslim. One of the main virtues a son of Allah must cultivate is generosity. You have been generous in giving up your freedom for your father. That says a lot about your character. You are part of my family, Ali, as if you were my son. You have earned it.

Therefore, I will cover the expenses of your father's release, and you owe me nothing. Don't worry. Your father and you are free men."

"Thank you, El Kaid, for your generosity, but I would like to repay that debt."

"You know I only have one word, and that has been said," the corsair pronounced firmly.

In the years he had been under the corsair's command, Ali knew he didn't like to argue, and when he made a decision, he didn't like to change it.

"Thank you. I am and will be grateful."

"We need to get him on a ship heading to the Canary Islands or Spain. I know there is a redemption planned in these days; it will be a great opportunity to get your father out of

Algiers. Unless you want him to stay here."

"No, he wants to go back to Gran Canaria. My mother is alone and needs his help."

"Then let's not talk about it anymore, Ali. This afternoon, we'll go to the port to resolve your father's departure. Let's go eat; I'm hungry."

"That sounds like an excellent idea. My father needs to rest and regain strength."

"By the way, it's time you bought or built a house in the city. To the west of my palace, there are good plots of land. Have you thought about that?"

"No, I haven't thought about it. I'm more focused on continuing to learn, little by little, until I become a corsair. I only need a cot to sleep in."

"You are already a corsair, Ali, and one of the good ones. A good corsair like you must have a decent place to start a family. You won't live forever on my ship or in Algiers's cheap hostels. Consider the idea, and when we return from the next voyage, we'll sit down and look for a good place to build your new home."

"That sounds great. My new home, here, in Algiers. We'll talk about it when we return, sir."

"It is settled, Ali. Let's eat," he said, clapping his hands to call the servants.

That same afternoon, El Kaid and Ali Simon found a ship chartered by the Trinitarians that would depart for Cadiz in a week and would take more than a hundred people who had paid the corresponding ransom to the Berber corsairs.

El Kaid covered the expenses of the trip and gave Juan Romero a bag with twenty gold coins from the Portuguese Crown. It would be enough to pay for the passage from Algiers to Cadiz and from there to Gran Canaria; besides, he would have enough to live on for several years.

Ali Simon thanked him for the gesture and said he would pay him back. The corsair told him never to forget the charity of the Muslims, that he didn't want to talk about that matter anymore, and that family matters were resolved within the family.

A surprise attack

After tying up loose ends in Algiers, they set sail once more towards the shores of Barbary. Onboard, the corsair El Kaid spoke to the young man:

"I've been contemplating raiding one of the Canary Islands for some months now, much like Turquillo or Calafat did. Such an attack could bring us great profits, especially through the sale of slaves. Boarding ships keeps us occupied and yields some benefit, but the real excitement lies in invasions. What do you think?"

"I believe we have a chance of success if we strike swiftly and by surprise. We could make an incursion into Lanzarote or Fuerteventura. Arriving, plundering a few villages, and seizing as many slaves as possible. These islands are poorly guarded by Castile. It would be suicide to attack Tenerife or Gran Canaria. They are heavily protected by the Canarian militias because the main ports supplying water and provisions to ships traveling to and from the New World are located there."

The young man's reasoning was sound. Both Gran Canaria and Tenerife were well defended by the forces of the Crown of Castile, and had repelled corsair and pirate incursions with some success. One of the most famous attacks was Pieter van der Does' assault on the city of Las Palmas, though he had to retreat due to the fierce resistance of the Canarians. In the battle, fourteen hundred people perished.

"Then let's set course for the Canaries. Once there, we'll decide whether to attack Lanzarote or Fuerteventura," declared El Kaid.

As days passed, the crew noticed the favor El Kaid showed towards Alí and the change in his status onboard over the past year. The corsair, without saying it explicitly, had granted special status to the convert because he believed he had the potential to become a great corsair and because he had a particular fondness for the Canary Islander. The crew knew this and dared not dispute such a decision.

After twenty days of navigation, they reached the shores of Lanzarote. They anchored in the channel dividing Lanzarote and Fuerteventura as they had arrived at dusk. Simón had been summoned by the old corsair. He descended into the cabin, knocked, and entered. El Kaid was reading the Quran.

"The Quran is a book that teaches many things. Its reading fills me with peace and tranquility before any battle. It should become your bedside book," he said without lifting his gaze from the sacred book.

"I've read some passages and I intend to continue, sir."

"It is crucial to know the Quran, Alí. A good Muslim must know it because it is the word of God, written by the Prophet Muhammad. I understand it may be difficult for converts to grasp. You were raised under a false religion, but you must strive to leave behind the commandments of the Christians."

"I understand, sir. I will endeavor to learn it with all my might, and I will succeed. Of that I am sure."

"I have no doubt, son."

"Have you decided which island to attack?" the convert asked.

"No. That's why you're here. I want you to decide," El Kaid replied.

"Me?" Alí asked incredulously.

"Yes, you. And I also want you to lead the attack."

"It's an honor, but also a great responsibility, and I'm not sure if I'm ready to take on that mission."

"Alí, I've known you for some years now, and I know you've been eager to carry out this task I entrust you with. Furthermore, I know you are prepared. You've learned a lot in these years. There's nothing left of the boy I took under my wing. Well, something remains, your courage, your integrity, and your determination."

"I must say, sir, it's a privilege that I'm not sure I deserve. However, since you've given me this opportunity, I won't let you down. I believe we should attack just before dawn to catch the natives off guard. No one expects an attack at that hour."

"So be it, Alí. You have command of the operation. Have you decided which island to attack?"

"Yes, sir. I have chosen the island of Lanzarote. The maps we seized from the Portuguese show that the city has a very calm beach where it will be very easy to enter with our boats. Additionally, we can get very close with our ship because there are no reefs."

"I see you haven't wasted time. You've studied the maps I gave you months ago."

"Yes, the Portuguese have good cartographers. Their maps are very detailed, and the notes on anchorages are magnificent. We should treasure them like true treasures, sir. They can serve us at any time and get us out of a few predicaments."

"Well, Alí, get moving. My ship is at your command," El Kaid said confidently.

He climbed up to the deck satisfied and ordered the boatswain to set course for the island of Lanzarote. His companion looked at him strangely. He made a gesture as if to say something, but thought twice and obeyed the orders of the Canary Islander without a word of protest.

Alí knew it was a great responsibility, that he could not fail, and that, with the success or failure of that attack, he would earn the respect of the rest of the corsairs. He only had the support of El Kaid and knew that some sailors were wary of his meteoric rise, although they did not express it in the presence of the old corsair because they knew he would not accept it. Not only was it a matter of demonstrating that he was a good strategist, but also showing them that he too could be a true leader. That was the day he had to show what he was made of.

Almost at dawn, they were anchored off the shores of the capital of Lanzarote. Alí Simón checked the strength and direction of the wind, which blew with enough force for the felucca to set sail the moment the Latin sails were hoisted. This detail was crucial to cover their escape route. If the operation didn't go as planned, they had to be prepared to set the ship in motion. For that reason, there was a crew of five sailors plus the boatswain ready to release the sails if necessary and set the felucca in motion.

The renegade corsair directed his men from the deck. He ordered them to prepare three boats and equip them with what was necessary for the incursion on the island's coast.

It was still before dawn when the three boats they had on board began to descend. Once in the water, they rowed towards the coast. Of the three boats, one was fully loaded with fifteen pirates led by Alí Simón, and the other two each carried a pair of pirates rowing towards the beach.

Only one lantern in each boat served as a guide, allowing them to see a meter or two ahead of their prows. The first boat was the one leading the way, guiding them to Arrecife beach.

They disembarked in silence, accompanied only by the sound of their own splashing and the breaking of the waves on the shore. Alí Simón divided them into three groups with clear orders: capture children, women, and young men; the old ones were to be left on land.

The attack would be swift

and precise. That depended on everything going as planned. They went from house to house, pulling out men, women, and children who screamed like mad as they were dragged from their homes and into the boats. The corsairs did not hesitate to use violence against any native who resisted. They were accustomed to such actions and knew how to ensure their missions were successful.

They left the shore with the same stealth with which they had entered it, rowing this time with greater speed to reach the felucca, which awaited them anchored offshore.

When the first rays of sunlight appeared on the horizon, the first soldiers guarding the city began to arrive, but not a single Barbary pirate remained on land, and they couldn't do anything against the corsairs' assault. All the soldiers saw clearly was Alí Simón's boat leaving the coast of Arrecife with ten natives on board accompanied by three pirates.

El Kaid was on deck observing the actions of his men. When Alí Simón was beside him, he said with a smile:

"I see the maneuver was quick and efficient. How many prisoners have we captured?"

"About forty, I'm not sure exactly. There was hardly any resistance, and what little we encountered, we subdued. The Spanish arrived so late that by the time they did, we were out of range of their muskets. You can see them from here. There are over thirty. If we had engaged in battle, much blood would have been shed, and many of us would have been fish food. There's no doubt they've reinforced the garrisons to protect themselves from our attacks. I think we need to consider abandoning the idea of attacking the islands and continue raiding ships. We can't afford such risks."

"You're right. From here, I can see it. They are equipped for combat. Thanks to your cunning, we have avoided a bloody battle. And it's true, I've heard in Algiers that many have attempted attacks on the islands; some have succeeded, and others have fled with their tails between their legs."

"Sir, let's set our bow towards a friendly port before a galley comes out to meet us," Alí Simón said firmly.

"Take care of distributing the captives, have them make a tally of how many there are, and treat them well. They are as valuable a commodity as the gold from the Americas. When you're done, set course for our port."

El Kaid left the deck and headed to his cabin, happy that his protege had emerged victorious in the first mission he had entrusted to him. He had not been mistaken. He felt proud to have a good nose for choosing sailors. He knew Alí Simón would go far and hoped to have him under his command for a long time. Having him by his side was a guarantee.

"Boys, take the captives to the holds and make sure they have both water and food. Ahmet, make a list of the exact number of prisoners. You know what to do."

With that said, Alí Simón gave the necessary orders for them to weigh anchor with fifty-five Lanzaroteans in the hold, who would be sold in the slave market of Algiers.

Some time after their incursion into Lanzarote, the corsair El Kaid appointed Alí Simón as his boatswain and right-hand man. Any decision of importance was consulted with the renegade because he knew his opinion was highly qualified and had to be taken into account.

Alí Romero felt satisfied because he had become a true corsair, and, most importantly, he not only had the support of his mentor but had earned the respect of his other companions.

An unfortunate meeting

After the captives captured in Lanzarote were sold, El Kaid insisted that the convert should buy a house; he would cover the expenses and pay them back gradually. Alí Simón reluctantly agreed; he didn't like having debts with anyone. However, he knew that the old corsair did it from the heart because he liked having him by his side.

He was aware that he needed a house. Algiers was his place of residence, and he was tired of the rundown hostels around the port. He needed a quiet and simple place, without many pretensions, a place to rest after long days at sea.

He was carried away by the enthusiasm of the Algerian corsair, and they settled on a single-story house that had belonged to a Berber pirate who had been ruined after a confrontation with a Spanish Armada ship and couldn't maintain the lifestyle he had led until then.

The house was near El Kaid's mansion, built on a plateau overlooking the port. It was made of limestone and had seven rooms and a bathroom at the back. What the Canary corsair liked the most was the entrance, formed by a large horseshoe arch that gave it a spectacular appearance.

They didn't take more than a week to complete the purchase and decoration of the house, which was taken care of by one of El Kaid's women. Alí Simón kept two captives from Lanzarote, Felisa and Francisco, to take care of the household chores.

After sorting out the affairs related to his new home, El Kaid and Alí Simón set off again towards Berbery. When they had been sailing for four days, they spotted a large three-masted sailboat heading towards the Canary Islands on starboard. El Kaid ordered them to set course towards the ship's figurehead; Alí Simón gave the appropriate orders for the sailors to get into a combat position; boarding was imminent. The thirty-five Algerian pirates armed themselves ready for battle, but before they could realize it, the first cannon shot was heard.

The projectile hit the bow, leaving behind a large hole and fatally wounding two crew members.

"Turn, turn! We're under cannon fire!" shouted Alí Simón.

He turned so fast that the second projectile fell into the sea, a few centimeters from the starboard side. They were fortunate that the old corsair ship was much faster in maneuvers, and the turns were executed more quickly. The ship continued to fire its cannons continuously, and the bullets whistled over their heads. The renegade saw how El Kaid observed his actions from the stern deck without missing a beat of the contest, as if he were attending a theatrical performance and the actions unfolding were not with him.

Against the third shot, Alí's maneuvers were insufficient; a black iron ball hot enough to shatter the jabeque's center. The Canarian was aware that it would not withstand another impact and would sink without remedy if another blazing ball hit it.

"To your posts! A fourth impact will send us to the bottom," shouted Alí Simón.

He made three consecutive turns while the cannon shots continued to fall to port and starboard without a single bullet hitting a plank of the ship's frame. It was the first time they had faced a ship with cannons, but they knew that in a direct confrontation they had nothing to do. In cases like this, there was only the possibility of fleeing, and that's what they did.

Berber ships were designed and built for boarding fishing boats or commercial ships and carrying out fleeting actions on coasts, on the beaches of islands and continents to capture prisoners. For this reason, they were light, with little draught, in order to be very fast. They also devoted a lot of time to preventive maintenance tasks to keep the sails and rigging in perfect condition, and during prolonged stays in port, they cleaned the hull of algae and crustaceans that lived on it.

This allowed them to avoid military ships, and when they spotted them, they changed course and lost them as soon as possible. But in recent times, some of these ships armed with more than twenty cannons per side disguised themselves as commercial ships and, on some occasions, managed to deceive pirates and corsairs.

Furthermore, due to the siege of corsairs and pirates, many merchant ships used between five and eight mobile cannons to protect themselves from attacks. Their handling was a very important deterrent element since, if they managed to hit the target before the corsairs boarded them, in most cases, they aborted the attack. But using a cannon was very complicated because it was a very difficult precision weapon to use. Only expert hands were able to hit the target at first try.

After ten consecutive turns, they managed to escape from the range of the ship's cannons. Alí Simón called the second boatswain and ordered him to set course for Algiers and, when fixed, to take stock of human losses and material damage.

The convert searched for El Kaid on the deck, but he couldn't find him. Upon reaching the stern of the ship, he saw the large hole made by the last projectile. That was where he had last seen him, right at the entrance to his cabin stairs. He stopped, looked down, and realized that the impact had hit the corsair's cabin full-on. Without thinking much, he jumped from above and, upon reaching the ground, found the body of his mentor from those years. He knelt before him and checked that his chest was shattered. A huge splinter of wood pierced his heart. He looked for a pulse in his neck, as the old corsair had taught him; however, he only found the silence of death.

He held back the tears, but then they flowed like a torrent on a stormy day, and he screamed with sorrow and rage. He calmed down, regained his composure. He breathed, went up on deck, and ordered the second boatswain to gather the corsairs at the stern.

Alí Simón waited for the men to be gathered in front of him. Most of them murmured; some talked among themselves. He checked with his eyes that most of them were there. He knew them very well. He had their faces engraved in his mind. He raised his hands with the palms turned downward and moved them up and down asking for calm.

The murmurs died down until only the flapping of the Latin sails, carried by the wind, and the sound of the hull jumping over the waves could be heard.

"I have to give you the worst news I never thought I would give you; our leader, El Kaid, has died," he paused trying to control the sorrow and anguish that choked him, "A wooden stake pierced his heart and split it in two."

The sailors started talking among themselves again. The Canarian corsair raised his hands again to calm the spirits of those present and said:

"We have lost a great man, one of the best I have ever known. You know what this man meant to me; he was my friend, my brother, and also my father."

He stopped to control the emotion that overwhelmed him. He felt his eyes moisten and fill with tears. He wiped them away with a slight gesture of his index fingers and continued:

"I will take command until we reach port. Once there, I will inform his relatives of his tragic end and leave this ship forever."

The murmurs of the corsairs returned to traverse the deck. They looked at each other without knowing what to do. El Kaid had been their leader for many years, a person to follow, a beacon to guide them in the darkness.

"But what are we going to do, what will become of us?" asked one of the younger sailors.

"The future is uncertain because we have lost our leader, who was also our friend, but life goes on and we cannot stop. We have to continue our course. We will shroud him and give him the burial he deserves. When we arrive in Algiers, we will talk. I promise you that none of you will be left without work. I give you my word."

The Canarian shrouded the Algerian's body. He undressed him and washed him completely, removing the blood stains that covered part of his body. He washed his head and beard; then he continued with the right side of the body and finished with the left. He cut the nails of his hands and feet. Then he covered him with three white cotton sheets, so that no part of him was left uncovered, and tied him with a hemp rope to hold the shroud fabrics.

He lifted him onto the deck with the help of three sailors and placed him on the starboard side. The second boatswain recited the first Takbir and the Sura Al-Fatiha. Then he continued with the second Takbir, with the third Takbir, and concluded with the fourth. He raised his hands and finished the ceremony reciting the Taslim.

They remained without saying a word until Alí Romero arranged the preparations to throw him into the sea following the old seafaring tradition. He stood behind his head, lifted him by the shoulders, and threw him into the sea. Alí watched the shrouded body float, as if it didn't want to be lost in the depths of the ocean, but shortly afterward, it sank, first by the feet, until his body was lost in the depths of the Atlantic.

The renegade thought that a new path was beginning here and that, with the death of his mentor, one door had closed, but another had opened. He smiled and said to himself, "Goodbye, friend, safe travels."

Upon reaching port, he went to find El Kaid's sons to personally communicate the news of their father's death and to deliver his most personal belongings and the jabeque to them.

With the death of the old corsair, he was freed from the commitment he had with him and with the entire crew. He addressed the sailors on the deck of the ship for the last time:

"Today I have delivered all the belongings to El Kaid's sons. None of his children want to continue with the corsair activity, so they have decided to sell the ship."

The second boatswain stepped forward and asked:

"What are you going to do, Alí?"

"I have some money, and with it, I want to build my own ship and become an independent corsair. Whoever wants to can join my crew. My doors are open."

Alí Romero knew what he wanted to do, and he worked hard to achieve it. From here, a new life began in which he would not be the only protagonist.

New direction

With the money he had managed to save during his years as a corsair, he negotiated the construction of a xebec in one of the many shipyards along the coast of the Mediterranean city. By the end of the year 1667, his splendid ship was floating in the capital waters of Algiers. He had achieved his great dream.

The following months were spent searching for materials to provision his ship and recruiting the sailors who would accompany him on his voyages. Most came on their own because word had spread that Ali Simon had a ship and was looking for competent corsairs. In the end, he acquired almost the entire crew that had sailed with El Kaid, which he supplemented with some Canary Islanders who had also renounced the Catholic religion and were good sailors.

In the spring of 1668, he unfurled the sails of his xebec, which he named The Canary, and set course for the coasts of Africa, where he began his solo corsair career.

His first corsair action took place off the coast of Gran Canaria, where he had been anchored for over five days. Ali Simon knew that sooner or later, some fishing boat would return along that route. He also knew that it was a risk to remain anchored in one place for so long. The corsair was aware that his survival depended largely not only on his selective attacks but also on being constantly on the move to avoid the formidable warships that patrolled the waters near the islands and the continent.

At noon on the fifth day, his boatswain shouted:

"Ship sighted on starboard! Ship sighted on starboard!"

Ali headed to the bow of the ship, grabbed his spyglass, and carefully observed his prey. It was a fishing boat that, upon noticing his presence, turned sharply to flee. Ali ordered the anchors to be hoisted, the sails trimmed, and set sail. The Canary began to sail, and before half a league had passed, it had reached its maximum speed.

The fishing boat tried to escape by making turns to port and starboard, but because its holds were filled to the brim with salted fish, its turns were slow, and its speed was not sufficient to escape the attack of the Canary.

After half an hour of sailing, Ali Simon ordered his men to prepare for boarding. The corsairs positioned themselves on the port side, ready with ropes and grappling hooks to initiate the boarding.

The Gran Canarian corsair took the helm and directed the approach maneuver. He positioned himself parallel to the fishing boat, turned slightly until the hulls made contact, and shouted:

"Boarding!"

The corsairs initiated the attack. Ropes with grappling hooks flew towards the deck of the fishing boat while Ali maintained his course to keep his xebec in contact with the fishing boat's hull. The shouts of the corsairs and fishermen mingled; some attacking and others trying to defend themselves.

The corsairs lowered the sails of the fishing boat, which, like a exhausted and defeated fish, came to a complete stop. After a few minutes of confusion, the corsairs seized the boat. Ali Simon jumped onto the fishing boat's deck, stopped in the middle, and remembered the fishing boat Las Ánimas when it was captured by El Kaid. He had a strange sensation remembering that past event. He barely remembered how much time had passed. His life changed completely that day, and he knew it had been a radical change, but a necessary one. He wondered what would have become of his life if he had never been captured by his mentor. He would never know. The truth was that he regretted nothing because he felt happy and powerful.

His men watched him wondering what was wrong. He took a few steps forward with his hands behind his back and asked:

"Who is the captain of this fishing boat?"

"That would be me, Simon."

It was strange to hear his Christian name while a man made his way through the corsairs and fishermen. It was the old captain Juan Sánchez. He had aged a lot, dragging his right leg and missing his left hand.

"Juan Sánchez?" asked the corsair, not recognizing the person in front of him.

"Yes, I am Juan Sánchez, although much older, with a nearly paralyzed leg, and missing a hand."

Ali approached, smiled, and said enthusiastically:

"It's been a long time, Captain. You finally managed to return home safe and sound."

"Yes, I was on a galley for over three years. We were rescued by a Spanish Armada ship, I returned to Gran Canaria, and a few months ago, an owner convinced me to return to these pirateinfested shores. You know, we have to eat and support our families. Besides, I am a man of the sea, like you, and I don't know how to do anything else. You've done well for yourself. I expected nothing less. When I saw you climb the mainmast of my old brig, I knew you would go far."

Ali smiled and approached the captain even more. He observed him closely. He had aged a lot. The three years rowing in the galley had left their mark. He looked into his eyes and said:

"Yes, Captain, I have done well. You know that hard work has its rewards. You are a fisherman, and I am a corsair. Both of us live off the captures. For that reason, we have to talk business. You will have your holds filled with fish; otherwise, you wouldn't be back."

"What are you going to do with us, Simon? You can keep all my captures and let us go to Gran Canaria, but don't take us to Algiers. I beg you. I can't bear to be back on a galley," pleaded the old fisherman.

"It's a good offer, Captain. You are a good, upright, and intelligent man, and also lucky."

"A lucky man, Simon? You are the lucky one. You are where you want to be and have achieved what you wanted. In contrast, here I am, maimed and lame. Bad luck has pursued me like a mangy dog since the day that corsair captured us."

"I'll put a price on your boat, your captures, and your crew. How does that sound?"

"What's that price? I'll never be able to pay you, Simon. You know that very well. I don't have a penny to my name."

"Choose your best man, and he'll come with me, Captain. That's the price. Neither more nor less."

The captain looked at his men. He knew who that man was, but he told the corsair:

"You know I can't do that, Simon. I won't hand over any of my men. None of them have a price. Not even for fifty xebecs would I sell them. They are my men, and on this boat, they're like my sons. Would you sell a son to save your own skin? No, right? Well, neither would I."

The corsair took the captain by the shoulders and said with a broad smile:

"I knew it! I knew you would give me that answer, Captain. Then there's no deal..."

"No, there's no deal, Simon. I don't want to go back to Algiers , but we don't write our destiny. Mine and my crew's are in your hands."

"No, Captain, you won't go back to Algiers, neither you nor any of your sailors."

Ali's boatswain shouted:

"Sir! Think it over! There's a lot of money at stake, and it's not a matter of throwing it overboard."

The canary looked at him sternly and told Juan Sánchez:

"Tell your men to transfer half of the salted fish to my holds, and when they're done, you can go. I hope not to find you again in these waters. You must retire, Captain."

"This was going to be my last season, but I'll have to go out again. In the half you keep is my retirement," he said reproachfully.

Ali looked up at the sky as if seeking an answer. He walked to the port side and felt the sea breeze caress his face. He breathed in and thought about what the old captain had told him, about the bad luck that had accompanied him since his capture by El Kaid and those years rowing in an infected galley that almost ended his life.

"Indeed, he's a good man and deserves a rest, Captain. The Quran teaches us to be grateful and to understand our fellow men. So, weigh anchor and set course for Gran Canaria. I won't keep anything. You're free, Captain."

The captain approached Ali Simon and said:

"Thank you, Simon. I knew one day you would go far, although I don't like what you do, gestures like this make you great, very great."

"You are a good man and deserve the winds, for once, to be in your favor. So go with your crew."

He turned on his heels, headed for his men, and shouted:

"It's time to abandon this ship, boys!"

The corsairs collected most of the ropes with the grappling hooks, leaving only two, and left the ship. The canary stood on the bow of the fishing boat, lost in thought. He saw Juan Sánchez being congratulated by his crew as if he had achieved a victory, but the captain knew they had been liberated by the generosity of the one who had been his cabin boy and had become a true corsair.

Ali crossed the deck to return to his ship, but before he could, Juan Sánchez grabbed his arm and said:

"I am in your debt, Simon. I don't know how I'll ever repay you for this gesture."

The Canary corsair thought about that debt and the image of his parents came to mind. He looked at the captain and said:

"Perhaps you can settle that debt in an easy way, Captain."

"Tell me how I can do it. If it's within my power, I'll gladly do it."

"You know my parents live in the Canary Islands, and I can't send them any money because the authorities on the island know its origin and confiscate it. I just want you to deliver the wages due to a sailor for this catch to my father. Can you do that?"

"Of course I can, Simon. I'll do it. "

Ali Simon extended his hand to the captain and said:

"Good luck, friend, and take care."

"I wish you the same."

The corsair took one of the ropes holding the boats together, propelled himself, and climbed onto his xebec. He ordered the ropes and grappling hooks to be released and set sail.

Ali Simon watched as the wind filled the sails of the fishing boat, its bow headed for Gran Canaria, disappearing over the horizon.

Then, he ordered them to set course for Barbary. When the xebec was in full sail, he approached his boatswain and said softly:

"I never make a decision without considering it. Don't ever question my authority again because the next time you do, I'll leave you in port. I need men who trust me. Is that clear?"

"I just thought you were letting your feelings get the better of you, sir."

"My heart travels with me, Mustafa. Never forget what the prophet has taught us. We must leave room in our hearts for charity, for doing good to our fellow men. Allah is great, and greater is his wisdom, Mustafa. If you're not comfortable with what I've said, you're free to do as you please."

The boatswain fell silent and set the course towards the African coast.

***

Certainly, here's the text without the long dashes:

As he seized ships and slaves, his fame spread across the ports of the Mediterranean and the Atlantic. Each time he left port, he returned with one or two captured sailboats and a multitude of slaves to sell at the Baths of Algiers.

ALI THE CANARY. A BARBARY CORSAIR

In December of that same year, Ali Romero arrived on the shores of Lisbon. They arrived towards evening and anchored seventy miles from the capital, away from the cannons of the fortresses and the Lusitanian galleons. As the day broke, one of his sailors spotted in the distance a large ship approaching from starboard; at the same time, they saw another vessel that was clearly a pirate.

The two pirate ships directed their bows towards the same target, as if following a preconceived plan. Ali Simon navigated zigzagging to starboard, and the other pirate ship, to port. The first cannon shots were heard from the ship to be raided, but the projectiles passed from one side to the other without hitting the hulls of the attacking ships.

Without waiting for any signal, the pirates took their positions to begin the boarding; they were only fifty meters from the English ship. The bow of Ali's ship headed towards the starboard side, and when there were no less than twenty meters left, the corsair veered sharply, leaving his vessel alongside the enemy ship. The pirates jumped onto the deck while from the port side, the other pirate did the same, boarding the left side of the English ship with his bow. In a few minutes, a tumultuous action dominated the entire deck of the ship along with shouts in many languages, sounds of muskets, pistols, and sabers. Not an hour had passed when the pirates had already seized control of the ship. Ali Simon slowly made his way towards the stern of the ship, where he encountered the other corsair who had helped him subdue the English ship, and said to him:

"My name is Ali Simon Romero, although many know me as Ali the Canary."

"I am Coralí."

"I've heard of you in the port of Algiers," Ali said.

"Your name is also known in the seas and ports through which I sail. I've heard that you sailed with the great El Kaid until he died in a confrontation in Berberia."

"Yes, El Kaid was a great man. May Allah have him in his glory. Everything I know, I learned from him. But we need to discuss how we will divide this substantial booty. It's the first time I've captured a merchant ship in collaboration with another corsair."

"Half for you and the other half for me, no more no less," Coralí declared.

Ali Simon thought that percentage was fair because both had collaborated equally to board the ship.

"So be it. It's fair."

Ali took a step forward and called the captain. When he saw him, he deduced that he was English and that they had boarded a ship of that nationality.

"Well, we have very little time. What do you have on board?"

"Passengers and cargo," he replied in a convoluted Castilian accent, rolling his r's.

"How vague. We need more information, captain, and I know you have it. I don't want to get angry because when I do, the sharks win."

At this, a voice emerged from the crowd speaking perfect Castilian:

"I demand that you lay down your weapons and let us continue our course. I speak on behalf of the Crown of Castile."

"With what high representation do I have the pleasure of speaking?" Ali Simon asked the crowd.

"With Don Lorenzo Santos de San Pedro, Regent of the Council of Seville, of the Royal Council, Lord of Baños, and of the Order of Santiago."

"It's an honor, sir," he said ironically, making a mocking bow, "but don't forget that in these seas, titles and royal names are of little value. They usually end up at the bottom of the sea. Here, the laws of men are superfluous, and the laws of corsairs and pirates prevail. Nevertheless, I'll tell your grace that you'll have the opportunity to assert your name and titles when demanding ransom. Corsairs are very understanding."

"But how is it possible that a Spanish nobleman has fallen so low as to engage in robbery and bribery?" the nobleman asked with an astonished expression.

"Many in Castile do the same: they steal, they bribe, and they kill. The only difference is that they are blessed by the Crown of Castile. We renegades, like my friend Coralí and I, have done it not out of greed but out of simple survival. We have been left with no choice but to turn to piracy."

"But the Crown..."

"Enough of your verbiage!" the Canary cut in with severity. "You'll have all the time in the world to make your demands; now worry about finding enough gold and silver to prevent you from ending up on a galley. A long journey to Algiers awaits us."

"And what do you call yourself? I don't want to forget your name."

"Ali Simon, better known as Ali the Canary."

"Ah, so it's you. I had heard that a renegade Canary was tarnishing the name of Castile and the Canary Islands."

"Don't concern yourself with my exploits or my fame; both are fleeting. Concern yourself with your neck. Mustafa! You know what to do. Don't forget anyone. Let them lack neither water nor food."

He approached Coralí and remarked:

"We've made a great capture, my friend. This seizure will bring us many benefits. Capturing a Regent of Castile doesn't happen every day. When we reach Algiers, we'll talk business. We can have a party at my house to celebrate this success."

"Yes, friend, we'll settle the division in Algiers, and I'll gladly attend that party. I've needed a good rest for a long time."

The capture of the Regent of the Royal Council of Seville brought him great benefits and increased his fame in the ports of the Mediterranean and the Atlantic. He was more than respected in Algiers.

He hosted a grand feast at the new mansion he had acquired on the outskirts of the city of corsairs, attended by the most renowned corsairs and pirates of Algiers and the highest representatives of the city. Ali Romero felt happy and proud.

Blood brother

During one of his resting periods, news reached him that his brother Salvador had been captured by a French ship after a bloody battle off the African coast, during which he had lost his right leg to a cannonball.

Seated in the hall of the new mansion he had acquired a few months ago, Ali Romero recalled the first time his brother arrived in Algiers with the intention of becoming a pirate. Ali Simon tried to persuade him, offering him a fishing boat to return to Gran Canaria and engage in coastal fishing, which could sustain his family and earn him an honest living. But Salvador refused and asked him:

"You tell me to earn an honest living when you are one of the greatest corsairs of the Mediterranean and the African coast? Why can't I be like you?"

"I had no choice. Life led me to what I am today. I'm offering you an alternative that I didn't have. If I had, I would be in Gran Canaria fishing."

"Forget about me, brother. Let me follow my own path. My destiny is written in the sea, and neither you nor anyone else will change my mind," his brother replied arrogantly.

"I won't be the one to stop you from doing what you want with your life, but I'm offering you a dignified way out, with which you can have a peaceful future and also help our parents."

"Thank you for the offer, but I've made up my mind. I'll embark on the first ship that accepts me."

"You're a fool. I'm offering you the opportunity to live peacefully for the rest of your life. If you engaged in coastal fishing, you could support not only your future family but also our parents. The risk would be minimal. You know better than I do that fishing a few miles off Gran Canaria poses no risk."

"How easy it is to speak from this magnificent mansion!" his brother retorted. "The life of a fisherman is very tough, and you know it. I don't want to spend my life salting fish and smelling of rotten entrails."

Ignoring his younger brother's advice, he took advantage of Ali Simon's trip to Turkey to apostatize, taking the name of Mustafa Arráez, and enlisted on a vessel to engage in piracy.

The voice of one of his servants brought him back from his thoughts. Ali Romero considered leaving his brother to his fate, but he didn't. He was blood of his blood and a good Muslim; he shouldn't turn his back on his own.

So he pulled the necessary strings to manage his brother's freedom, paid the ransom, and within a month, he had him by his side. He hosted him in his house, and one day, two weeks after his rescue, during dinner, they revisited the matter. Ali Simon said:

"Salvador, it's necessary for you to return to the Canary Islands," he said, his expression very serious.

"Call me Mustafa. You know I'm a Muslim, like you."

"Very well, brother Mustafa. I repeat, you have to go back to our parents. They need you. Besides, you have one less leg. No one will want you as a corsair. A cripple is not a good sailor and is not welcome on a ship. Your adventure is over."

His brother left the cutlery on the table and said:

"Perhaps you should be the one to return to our parents, Ali. You have enough money to support them for the rest of their lives. Besides, stop meddling in my life. I am the only one responsible for my actions."

"Don't think I haven't considered it. Going back to Gran Canaria. Many times I dream of it. Being at peace and just living, but those are just dreams. I can't go back anymore. When I set foot in Las Palmas, they will arrest me, judge me as a heretic, and burn me at the stake in any public square. In contrast, you can go back. No one knows you, and your head is not on the line. You are free to return. Only our parents are waiting for you."

"I'm not going back, brother. I plan to enlist as soon as I can. I want to make a fortune like you, have a mansion like this, retire with seven wives, and live like a bey. That's my dream, and I won't stop pursuing it."

Ali Simon couldn't understand his brother's insistence on remaining a pirate. There was no way to change his mind.

"Life isn't that easy. I've been lucky, very lucky. I had the honor of learning from one of the wisest corsairs Algiers has ever known, and yet, a cannonball shattered his heart into two pieces. You've had your first warning. Take advantage of the opportunity I offer you and leave, return to our parents."

"No, Ali. I appreciate your offer, but I have a good feeling. I know I'll go far. I'll become more important than you, my name will be remembered and sung by the bards of the Mediterranean villages."

"I won't repeat it. You're the master of your own destiny. What I will tell you, so you're clear, is that I won't pay for your rescue again. If you get captured again, face the consequences, Mustafa."

"I know. Don't worry, soon I'll pay you every last ounce of gold or silver you've paid for me. I don't like having debts, especially not to you."

"You're my brother, and I won't charge you for your rescue. It would be indecent. Let's eat."

"I don't want your charity, Ali. I'll pay you what I owe you."

Ali Romero didn't reply, and they continued eating. The corsair had a feeling that this would be the last time he would see his brother and felt saddened. He didn't understand his brother's attitude and his eagerness to achieve the successes he had achieved.

He told him that he wouldn't rescue him again, and he kept his word. A year after his first rescue, he was captured again, this time by a Spanish warship. He was condemned by the Inquisition of Granada, which unsuccessfully tried to exchange him for some Christian captives upon learning that his brother was a famous corsair.

The missive from the Bishopric of Granada reached him through a Trinitarian monk who was in Algiers preparing one of the multiple redemptions they carried out in that city.

Ali received him one afternoon in the hall of his mansion. The monk was a young lad of barely twenty years old. He wore a white tunic with a large red and blue cross at chest height and a huge rosary that reached from his waist to his left knee.

The Trinitarian entered slowly, following Francisco, one of the Canarian servants of the corsair, who led him to where Ali Simon was.

"Good afternoon, sir. May God bless this house and all your family."

"Thank you. May Allah also bless you and yours."

The corsair invited him to sit and then instructed Francisco to serve him hot mint tea with a little brown sugar.

"I'm here on behalf of the Bishopric of Granada to make a captive exchange a reality. I present you with the personal letter of the Bishop of Granada," he said, handing the letter to Ali Romero. "If you'd like, I can read it to you if you don't have that privilege."

Ali didn't answer; he took the letter and read it. When he finished, he said to the young monk:

"This isn't the first time I've paid for my brother's release, and this time I won't do it."

"This time it's a simple exchange. You're a man of great influence in this city, Mr. Ali Romero, and you won't have any difficulty in having the ten Granadan captives released who are mentioned in the bishop's letter."

What the young religious said was true. He wouldn't have any trouble doing what the bishop asked of him. If you had enough money, you could free whoever you wanted. However, that wasn't the problem.

"I know I wouldn't have difficulties in doing what the bishop asks of me. This very afternoon, I would have the matter resolved. You know it; if you have enough money, you can release whomever you propose.

However, sir, that's not the case; I have the influence and money to make that happen, but, as I told you, I won't do it."

"But for God's sake! He's your brother, blood of your blood. You know better than anyone that if you don't agree to this exchange, he's likely to be condemned to die at the stake as a heretic or to die in a galley of the Kingdom of Castile."

The friar didn't need to tell him what he knew. Ali stood up, took the tea cup, and took a sip. Then he replied:

"I won't allow you to judge me, especially not in my own house. My brother is solely responsible for his current situation. What you don't know is that I begged, not to say pleaded, for him to stop playing at being a corsair, especially after he lost a leg in a confrontation with a ship. I paid his ransom, managed to bring him to these lands, but I didn't convince him to return to my land, to the Canaries. He ignored my advice, even my money. I swore to him that if he was captured again, I wouldn't intercede for him, and that's what I'll do. My brother is a fool who deserves what has happened to him. Arrogance, envy, and greed are bad traveling companions. In the end, they devour your insides."

The Trinitarian finished his tea because he knew it would be the only warm thing he would have for a long time. He stood up and said:

"I see there's nothing to negotiate. You're abandoning your brother to his fate. From what I've gathered, good fortune never accompanied him. I only tell you that if you change your mind, we'll depart in two days. You know where to find us. Thank you very much for receiving me, and may God the Father watch over your actions and your family."

Ali Simon remained silent. Then he said to the monk:

"May Allah be with you, sir."

He clapped twice, Francisco entered, and he said:

"Francisco, prepare our cart and take the Trinitarian to the port."

"Thank you, Mr. Ali Romero."

The corsair sat back down and poured himself some more tea. The image of his brother returned to his mind as if he were a ghost from the past. He felt sad because he didn't like what he was doing. A part of him screamed to go to his brother's aid, to save him from certain death, but another part told him that his brother got what he deserved, that if he rescued him again, he would never be grateful. He would embark on another corsair adventure guided by his pride and greed, and he would never acknowledge his help because his pride would prevent him.

After his encounter with the Trinitarian monk, he never heard from his brother Salvador again until he received news from a French pirate who had requested work from him. This pirate told him:

"I knew who he was when he revealed that he was the brother of the great Ali the Canary. We rowed together, shoulder to shoulder, for almost a year on a French galleon. During those long days when we rowed until exhaustion, we talked about you and your insistence that he stop being a pirate. He confessed to me that he regretted it and that he should have followed your advice and accepted the offer you had made him.

In the end, he knew that being in a galley was the worst sentence that could befall a man because over time, if you weren't released, you lost your life without remedy. You're rowing one day and the next without rest. You see the dawn rowing, and at nightfall, you keep rowing. Day after day like this. Then there are the lashes from the overseers, who tear your skin to shreds. They're watching and ready to use the whip, which they constantly make sound to remind you that if you dare to stop, it will sound like lightning on your back. And to keep you like a dead man walking, they give you a morsel of bread soaked in wine or vinegar, and, at best, a bite of barley porridge with olive oil. When I was freed, your brother was famished, almost without the strength to row. When he left that filthy galley, he could hardly stand on his own. I don't think he survived. Few survive the galleys."

Ali listened to the story with a serious and troubled expression, but his brother had decided to follow the dictates of ambition and greed, and those paths ended in perdition.

Ali thought of his brother, and sadness overwhelmed him because he believed he could have paid his ransom and perhaps convinced him to return to their parents. He had been consumed by his own pride. He locked himself in his room, prayed for him, and begged Allah to keep him alive. However, he never heard from him again.

The Bishop

The Bishop Bartolomé García Ximénez Rabadán was in his quarters at the episcopal see, writing a letter to his brother.

Dear Mateo,

Thank God, I have finally arrived at the episcopal see of the Diocese of Canarias and Rubicón in Gran Canaria after sixteen months of misfortune upon misfortune. I am writing to you so that there is a record of it because, when I tell the story, it's hardly believed. It seems like this journey was cursed by the devil from the moment of my appointment as bishop.

We departed from Cádiz on July 5th, 1665, aboard a well-equipped Genoese saetía with three masts and six immense square sails that nearly lifted the ship off the water. In the early days, it seemed like we were on a good course. Then, the captain informed us that we had veered off course and ended up at the Azores, but we still had a chance to correct it and resume the right heading. I remember seeking him out on the deck and asking:

"But, how did we veer off course, master? Aren't you a man of the sea?"

"It was a misreading, Your Eminence."

"A misreading? I don't understand."

"A misreading of the stars. We've been sailing five nights with the wrong heading, but I've corrected it and we're now headed towards the Canaries."

"I hope so because I need to be in the Islands by the scheduled date to assume my position. There's much work to be done on those isles."

"Don't worry, Your Lordship, we'll arrive three or four days later than planned, but no more."

I prayed with all my might for this to be the case, but God, in His mercy, did not heed my prayers because we inexorably arrived at the shores of Africa, where we were nearly captured by Berber corsairs sailing those infidel coasts.

Faced with this panorama, I confronted the captain again, observing the land on the horizon:

"We've finally arrived."

The captain did not respond and continued gripping the helm.

"Captain, did you not hear me? Have we arrived?"

The master released the helm and responded with a serious expression:

"No, Your Eminence, that land you see ahead is Africa, and those ships you see beyond the horizon are corsairs and pirates."

"Jesus, Mary, and Joseph! Corsairs and pirates? May God have mercy on us! I don't want to end up in the Baths of Algiers."

"Don't worry, they haven't seen us, and we're moving away from them."

"Don't worry? Let me tell you, captain, I never thought I'd find myself in this situation. This ship and this journey are cursed. I deduce that you've once again made a mistake. At this rate, I'll arrive in the Canaries to celebrate the Nativity of Jesus Christ, our Lord."

The sailor fell silent as if he didn't know what to say. I think he was aware that he had lost his way.

"Again blaming the elusive stars?" I asked mockingly.

"Navigation is a very complicated science, Your Lordship. Not only must one read the courses correctly in the stars, but one must also know the currents and interpret the charts accurately. I am convinced that the reading of the night sky was correct. This time the current has been carrying us towards the African coast almost unnoticed. It's an almost invisible process that inexorably leads you in another direction. That's what happened to us."

"What are you telling me? That we've missed the Canaries?"

"I'm afraid so, Your Eminence, but don't worry. According to my calculations, the Islands are to the north. I'm sailing in that direction, and in a few days, we'll be in the port of Las Palmas."

"By the blessed God!" I exclaimed in astonishment. "We've been sailing for twenty-five days when we thought we'd arrive in ten or fifteen to the Blessed Isles. You yourself told me so."

"Your Lordship, the situation is under control, we are now on the right course."

"I'm not so sure if we are, captain. I don't trust your nautical knowledge. You've been wrong twice. I have more and more doubts that you'll manage to bring us to a safe harbor. All we can do now is pray and let God guide you among the stars and the ocean currents because otherwise, we'll end up in the very depths of hell."

The captain attempted to return to the Canaries, but the strong winds forced us to set a course for America. Yes, America, Mateo. The master gathered us on deck and delivered some grim news:

"I have to give you some bad news."

A murmur ran through the group, and he continued with his speech:

"The strong northern currents prevent us from reaching the Islands, and, coupled with the lack of wind, the ship cannot sail any further towards them. Therefore, I have decided to follow the path marked by the current, which will undoubtedly take us towards America."

"America?" I asked almost shouting. "Have you gone mad, captain? I demand that you stick to the established plan and return us to the Canary Islands."

"It's impossible. The currents prevent it. Besides, at this point, it's easier to reach the Americas than any island in the Canaries, not to mention that we could die in the attempt. So that's the decision."

After the group dispersed, I went straight to speak with him:

"This journey is not cursed, sir, you are incompetent and don't know what you're doing. I will file a formal complaint with your shipowner, and I will ensure that you never captain a ship again. What do I say, not even a rowboat. You are unaware of the harm you are causing to the Church. With your absolute lack of nautical judgment, you have abandoned countless parishioners who were eagerly awaiting the assumption of their new bishop."

"I cannot fight against the elements."

"The elements, sir? Don't fancy yourself as King Philip II. You lost your way from the moment we left Cádiz, and you have no idea where your right hand is, let alone how to reach the Canary Islands. I pray to God the Father that he guides us, that he takes the helm and leads us to a safe harbor."

We entrusted ourselves to God the Father when the provisions began to run low. He gathered us again on deck, and it wasn't good news. I looked around, and we were all there. Only then did he begin to speak:

"From today onwards, we will begin rationing food at a rate of eight ounces every twenty-four hours. Water will be treated similarly, half a glass three times a day. The sailors may drink double, as they are working and need water to continue their tasks."

Upon hearing his words, I said angrily:

"The situation is going from bad to worse. Not only are we lost in these godforsaken seas, but we are also going to add the hardships of hunger and thirst. As they say in my homeland: if we were few, now the grandmother has given birth. At least tell us that we will reach the shores of America, even if it's starving and thirsty."

"Don't exaggerate, Your Eminence, the course is correct, and in a few days, we'll be in the lands that

Columbus discovered."

"May God hear you and do it soon because, if we go by the facts, we'll end up in the China of the illustrious Marco Polo without a doubt."

I prayed every day for the evil fate to finally leave us and the clutches of the devil to release our ship.

God heard my pleas and sent us the ship La Trinidad—the Father, the Son, and the Holy Spirit—to save us from an uncertain end that could have ended in certain death.

We received Captain Baltasar de Recuesta of La Trinidad on the aft deck. I approached him and said joyfully:

"Thank God we have found you; if it hadn't been for that, we would have perished. We had hardly any food or water left."

"What part of America was your destination, Your Excellencies?"

"Captain," I said, taking the floor again, "our original destination was the Canary Islands..."

"The Canary Islands? But how did you end up here? Did you encounter a storm that diverted you from your destination?"

The captain of the saetía remained silent, knowing that what had happened to them had no explanation.

"No," I replied ironically. "Here our supposed captain, king of the South Seas, made a wrong turn, and we arrived at the Azores. Then, we arrived in Africa, sailed past the Canaries, and the ocean currents forced us to continue to the Americas. Quite an odyssey that deserved to be written by Homer himself and become part of the annals of navigation history."

The captain of the ship said:

"Now you are safe. According to our calculations, we are two days from the island of Puerto Rico. There you can rest and regain your strength. Subsequently, you can embark on a ship bound for Castile, which will surely make a stop at some Canary Island to replenish water and provisions necessary to continue your journey."

"I hope the Holy Lord hears you, and that we arrive safe and sound in Puerto Rico because it is true that we are exhausted and need rest to regain the necessary strength to sail back to the Blessed Isles."

"Don't worry, Your Excellency, you are in good hands. If you wish, we have a free cabin aboard La Trinidad where you can sleep and regain strength until we reach solid ground."

"You don't know how much I appreciate it. I will pray for you five Hail Marys and five Our Fathers. La Trinidad is a blessing from heaven."

Joy filled our hearts as we stepped onto the solid ground of the island of Puerto Rico on the 9th of August in the same year of the Lord. After replenishing our strength and eating proper meals, we set sail once again to assume my position in the Canaries. The scheduled departure date was the 10th of October, and we embarked on a caravel that, once out of the shelter of Puerto Rico's calm waters, proved to be quite challenging to navigate. Oh, how we missed the Genoese saetía.

After five days at sea, I traversed the deck, clinging to any available element for support. I sought out the ship's pilot and found him at the helm. Approaching him, I inquired, "Why does this ship move so much, master?"

"Caravels are very seaworthy vessels, Your Excellency. They are sturdy and sail well, but they pitch and roll a lot. What about Columbus? He used three ships like these to discover the Americas. However, they are designed for experienced sailors, men of the sea accustomed to wind and waves. Passengers without maritime experience often struggle. In my cabin, I have bags of ginger root. It will help you. It's infallible against seasickness. Do not hesitate to take a piece and chew on it. It will be spicy, but endure the heat. I fear the sea is growing rough. Do you see those dark clouds on the horizon, how the wind blows, and the waves begin to break on the bow?"

"Yes, captain, I see them," I replied with a certain fear.

"Well, that signals a very strong storm. When it hits us, our ship will become a mere nutshell at the mercy of the wind and waves. Pray, Your Excellency. Pray to God to deliver us from this. You know more about prayers than I do. We will try to keep the ship afloat, to prevent it from sinking and becoming fresh meat for the sharks."

"But Lord Jesus," I implored, looking to the sky, "what have I done to deserve this? What more trials must I endure to prove myself worthy of such a destiny?"

"I heard your story in the port. What a journey, Your Excellency! From Cádiz to the Canaries, passing through the Azores, Africa, and Puerto Rico. The captain was a novice. It was his first time on such a voyage."

"A novice? But how could they entrust such a responsibility to an inexperienced person?"

"You know what they say: 'You learn to castrate by cutting eggs,' and everyone has a first time. But don't blame him entirely. The responsibility lies with the shipowner who placed the helm in his hands knowing he had no experience. Some shipowners are irresponsible and, for the sake of profit, will do anything."

"Are you not a novice?" I asked, fearing the impending storm.

"Do I look like one, Your Excellency?"

I examined him closely. He had gray hair, a beard that reached his chest, and a large scar across his right eye that disappeared into his beard.

"No, you seem to be a man well-versed in these matters."

"I stepped into a boat at the age of three. My father was a fisherman, Your Lordship, and since then, I have not stopped sailing. At twenty, I began to captain a fishing boat, and at twenty-four, I crossed the Atlantic in a caravel like this one. I've been back and forth from Cádiz to America and vice versa ever since."

"We can rest assured because we are in good hands."

"The first thing a sailor must learn, Your Excellency, is that one can never be at ease at sea. The sea is a beast that is mostly asleep, but when it awakens, one must be prepared. It is waking up, so go below and do not come on deck until the storm subsides. And remember the ginger; you will need it."

The devil's claw continued to wreak havoc. He was determined that I would never reach the Islands to assume the distinguished task of the bishopric of the Blessed Isles and that I would perish in the depths of the ocean. Yes, Satan was behind the storm that engulfed us at sea. I remembered the captain's words and the nutshell metaphor. The ship swayed from side to side, making it impossible to stand upright. The safest place was the hammocks, keeping us away from our belongings, which were tossed from one side of the ship to the other without order or control. The ginger made the discomfort caused by seasickness almost nonexistent, and vomiting did not occur. Some passengers who refused to take the medicinal root fell prey to nausea and uncontrollable vomiting.

The storm passed, and calm returned. I climbed onto the deck and surveyed the damage the wind and waves had inflicted upon the caravel. I sought out the captain and found him tied to the helm with a rope. He seemed like a wounded animal or a father who had lost a child. I approached and asked him, "What has the storm left us?"

He took a moment to reply. Turning around, he released the rope that kept him tethered to the helm and said, with a gaze lost on the wet planks of the deck, "I lost three of my men. A giant wave swept them away, and we lost them forever."

"By the blessed God! May God have them in His glory!"

"Furthermore, one of those giant waves tore the rudder blade off completely. So, we are without control, adrift, at the mercy of the ocean currents that will take us who knows where, Your Excellency."

I could not believe what my ears were hearing. Once again, the devil had placed his foul claw in my path, so I asked the experienced captain, "Is there no solution to regain control of the ship?"

"There is a solution, Your Lordship. It involves constructing a makeshift rudder, which as the name suggests, will serve to mitigate our drift. But we are at the mercy of fortune and of God. So now I ask you to pray, Your Excellency, to pray with all your might because we need the Almighty's help more than ever."

"I will pray until I am hoarse, I assure you. You try to fashion that makeshift rudder; I will entrust myself to God."

At noon, we prayed the Holy Rosary for the souls of the three deceased sailors. Then we continued praying. The captain decided to ration food and water because we did not know how long we would be lost at sea.

Once again, I implored God to send the Holy Trinity to defeat the devil, and He heard my prayers because a few days later, we spotted a fleet of English merchant ships that rescued us. They demanded an exorbitant sum for the rescue, and we had to pay them fifteen hundred pesos and the chalice, the paten, the pectoral cross, the ring, and even the tobacco boxes. It is known that Lutherans are not good Christians, and many, like these Englishmen, are driven more by pure greed than by helping others.

We arrived in Tenerife on the 29th of December 1665, nearly six months after setting foot on Canary soil. I was bedridden for some time; many made bets, saying I would not make it to the Epiphany of the Lord. However, God is merciful and granted me the health and strength necessary to continue with my pastoral responsibility.

Then I had to travel to the Tenerife town of Garachico to resolve a revolt led by some clergymen protesting issues related to Malvasia wine. Winemakers feared that the English would seize the entire production and monopolize the wine market. The General Captaincy had to intervene to quell the rebellion, but in the meantime, the winemakers, disguised as clergymen, over three hundred of them, raided the English cellars and put an end to their monopolistic ambitions in one fell swoop.

Satan had not erased me from his malevolent list, dear brother, and he had prepared the greatest trial I have ever faced in my long life.

After officiating the corresponding masses for All Saints' Day, I prepared to have dinner, and as you know, Matthew, I have a fondness for soft-boiled eggs, which to me are a king's delicacy. My personal secretary served me dinner. The two eggs were open at the top because that's how the cook prepared them, and I proceeded to enjoy the first one. I added some salt, slurped it up, and then finished it with some bread, aided by a silver spoon. It was delicious, cooked to perfection. I treated the second one in the same manner. However, as I slurped it, I noticed a strange, sour taste, as if it were spoiled, and I was alarmed to see that the silver spoon had turned a dark gray, almost black. Frightened, I called my secretary, ringing the bell and shouting:

"Miguel, Miguel!"

He entered the dining room in a hurry because I rarely called him so alarmingly, and asked, "What's wrong, Your Excellency? Are you alright?"

"I believe this egg is spoiled or something has been added to it," I said, as he took the egg and brought it to his nose to smell it. "This doesn't smell right, Your Excellency. Have you ingested any of the egg?"

"Yes, Miguel. Just a sip, no more."

"Try to vomit, Your Excellency. Stick your fingers down your throat and induce vomiting. It's the only way to expel the possible toxin."

I tried to do as my secretary had instructed, but all I managed to do was induce three or four retches that did not achieve the desired result. Then, Miguel said:

"With your permission, Your Excellency, kneel down; I'll have to do it for you. I see no other way to rid your stomach of the poison."

I complied without delay because something inside me told me that my life depended on it. So, I knelt down, and Miguel inserted his fingers into my throat so deeply that, after the first retch, I vomited. I breathed to regain my composure, and I heard my secretary say:

"We must repeat the operation, Your Excellency; we must cleanse your stomach thoroughly."

I let him proceed, Matthew, and I vomited five times until there was nothing left inside me. I drank some water to rinse my mouth and spat it out because I trusted nothing and no one, only my secretary.

Miguel took me to the doctor who, thank God, lived nearby, and he administered a series of antidotes that took effect. He said that undoubtedly what saved my life were the vomits induced by my secretary, which expelled most of the poison.

After due investigations, we learned that the poison was soliman, a compound of chlorine and mercury used to polish gold and silver, but which is deadly if ingested by humans.

The inquiries led us to a young kitchen assistant who confessed that a cleric had paid him a few silver coins to exchange one of the eggs for the poisoned one. The said cleric had been imprisoned for rebellion against the ecclesiastical establishment, and when he served his sentence, he devised the wicked plan. He was retried and sentenced to many years in prison. Later, I heard that he had escaped and left Gran Canaria.

I have been left with sequelae from the poisoning attempt, Matthew. Every morning I wake up with severe headaches that gradually subside throughout the day thanks to some infusions recommended by the doctor. I also have lifelong eczema on my forearms and calves, which I try to alleviate with an aloe vera poultice that works wonders.

As of today, Matthew, the situation is calm, and it seems that God has defeated the evil one, and I can dedicate myself body and soul to my pastoral work.

May God the Father watch over you and yours. I hope to see you soon, brother.

***

The bishop folded the six pages he had written, put them into an envelope, sealed it, and left the pen on the desk, reflecting on the odyssey he had lived through to reach the bishopric seat, events he would never forget. A deep sigh escaped him, and he rose from the table. He checked the time on the pendulum clock and prepared to have breakfast.

After an hour, he began to address the matters on his agenda. The bishop's secretary indicated the topics he had to deal with that morning, and one issue caught his attention: "Situation of the Canarians enslaved in Algiers. Convert Simon Romero Arráez, better known as Ali Simón or Ali the Canarian."

After finishing the first six items, the matter of the convert came up. A couple over sixty entered. The secretary invited them to sit in the two chairs arranged in front of the desk.

Bishop Rabadán waited for the couple to settle in, then said with interest, "You may speak."

"Good morning, Bishop," the man began. "My name is Miguel Quintana Martel, and my wife's name is María Auxiliadora Márquez Morales. We are here to ask for your help regarding the liberation of our son, Miguel Quintana Márquez, who was enslaved three months ago on the shores of Barbary. We know that he is enslaved by a renegade named Ali Simón, whose Christian name is Simón Romero Arráez, born and raised in Triana Street. We know that his parents are alive and that they reside in the same street. We have tried to get them to intercede for our son, but we have made no progress. They say they can't do anything because they hardly have any contact with their son, although we know they are receiving money from him. We thought that perhaps with the mediation of Your Excellency, we could achieve our son's freedom. We are poor people, with no resources, and we fear that this devilish Moor will end up selling our son, and we will never see him again. We know that, from time to time, there are redemptions in which Christian slaves are released by paying, and as we have said, we have nowhere to turn."

The bishop took notes as the elderly couple spoke. When they finished, he said, "I understand the problem, and I know that without money involved, the situation is difficult. I am also aware of the precarious situation of many families in these lands, which we are trying to alleviate with the Christian charity of those who have more. The first thing I will do is meet with the father of the convert to see if I have better luck than you, and I will try to find a solution that is nothing other than the liberation of your son."

"We also know of eight families in our same situation. You know that it is common to end up knowing people who suffer the same ailment, and in our case, it has been so. Here we have a list with the names of the captives in Algiers of all the families we have contacted," Miguel Quintana said, handing the bishop a list of the Canarian slaves that Ali Simón was supposed to have.

The bishop took the paper and read it calmly. He raised his head and said, "Today I will write a letter addressed to the father of the convert. I hope to have a meeting with him sometime this week or early next week. Go with God; I hope to have some response soon. Pray for your son; God is merciful and will watch over him."

"Thank you, Your Excellency."

After the customary farewell, the couple left the room, and the bishop reread the list of captives they had given him. He drafted a summons for Ali Simón's father and handed it to his secretary to process.

The following Friday, Juan Romero arrived at the episcopal headquarters. He entered the bishop's office behind the secretary, sat down, and waited for the prelate to speak. After finishing signing some documents, the bishop raised his head and said, "Good morning, Juan."

"Good morning, Your Excellency."

"You may wonder why I have summoned you."

"Yes, but I have a slight idea. I believe it has to do with some matter related to my son, Simon."

"Yes, the issue I want to discuss with you is directly related to your son. I understand that your son has apostatized from the Catholic religion and has embraced Islam."

"Yes, it's a fact that I don't like, but that's the reality."

"I also know that he has become a very famous corsair in Algiers and that he has several Canarian slaves under his custody."

"Simon was captured on the coasts of Barbary some years ago when he was just a boy. He was taken in by the corsair El Kaid. Now he engages in piracy and has his own ship, which he has named El Canario. I don't know if he has Canarian slaves in his custody."

"We know he does, Juan. Here is the list," the bishop said, handing him the written list of the Canarian slaves that Ali Simón was supposed to have.

The father took the paper, held it in his hands, handed it back to the prelate, and said, "I can't read, sir."

"That's alright, Juan. I just want you to intercede, to speak with your son to release these slaves," he said, indicating the list of slaves.

"I can do little, Your Excellency. I hear from him once a year, and sometimes I have no news of how his life is going. I send him one or two letters a year through a French ship that has safe conduct in Algiers, allowing it to enter its port without problems."

"Don't you send him money?"

"No, sir. The authorities know who my son is and what he does. If they had any news that I receive money, they would not hesitate to embargo it."

"In a way, that would be fair, wouldn't it? It's money bathed in pain and suffering, even blood."

"Yes, it's clear, Your Excellency."

"Would you be willing to send him a letter in my own handwriting?"

Ali Simón's father fell silent and then said, "I prefer that you do it. Your Excellency has more means than I do to make that shipment. As I said, I have no means. Besides, it has been almost a year and a half since I heard anything from my son. What I could do is have them write to him on my behalf to release those captives."

"That would be fine, Juan. I am convinced that it will have some effect. You don't know it, but those people are extremely poor. They have nothing to eat, let alone pay for a ransom. I will accompany my letter with yours. What do you think?"

"Whatever you do will be well done, Your Excellency."

"As you do not know how to write, I will instruct my secretary to take your fingerprint and imprint it on your letter. Then I will draft it. Thank you on my behalf and on behalf of those unfortunate families. You are a thread of hope."

"You can count on my help. I will do what I can."

"I reiterate my thanks, Juan."

The bishop rang a bell, and the secretary entered. He instructed him on what to do and began to draft the letter he would send to Simón Romero Arráez

The bishop's letters

Upon his return from one of his many voyages, and while in his mansion in the company of Isabel, a wealthy and beautiful merchant from Cadiz with whom he shared table, business, and, on occasion, some flirtatious moments, a letter arrived from Gran Canaria. He thought it might be a missive from his father, with whom he corresponded.

Francisco, a Canary slave in his service, said to him as he handed over the letter:

"It has arrived from Gran Canaria. It bears the bishop's seal."

He opened the envelope and found two letters, one from his father and another from the Bishop of the Canaries, D. Bartolomé García Ximénez de Rabadán. He read his father's letter first and then the one from the prelate, which said:

Esteemed Simon:

I pray to God that upon the arrival of this letter, you find yourself in good health. I have dared to address you because I have received more than ten letters from relatives of captives, children of God and faithful Catholics, who inform me that they are in your service. They also tell me that you are a man of good heart and that, in good faith, you have lent them money so they can purchase their freedom and thus prevent them from being sold to God knows what infidels from those lands of Islam.

My intention is no other than to intercede for these unfortunate souls so that, in one way or another, they may be returned safe and sound to their families.

I want you to indicate to me the way or ways in which we can negotiate the mentioned liberation.

I would not like to end without mentioning a point that distresses me and that I would like you to consider carefully and calmly. The matter is none other than your apostasy, which concerns and occupies me as the shepherd of the souls of these lands. I know that renouncing the Catholic faith must have been a meditated and difficult decision because it is to renounce one's own roots. I want you to reconsider the matter.

I await eagerly your response.

May God keep you and yours.

Canary Islands, June 15, 1686

His companion waited for Ali Simon to read both letters and then asked him:

"Now you're corresponding with bishops, dear Ali?"

"I am as surprised as you are, dear Isabel. Bishop Bartolomé García Ximénez de Rabadán asks me to free the slaves under my protection and urges me to return to the Christian faith I once followed."

"And what do you intend to reply?" asked the woman from Cadiz with interest.

"You know my thoughts on the matter of slaves, Isabel. It's the way I earn my living. I know no other."

"I've often thought your behavior towards the Canary slaves is strange. More than strange, peculiar. You're the only corsair I know who buys captives and keeps them under his protection. You have quite a number here, and I believe that half of them would be more than enough to maintain your mansion. I wonder why you buy them in the Baths of Algiers."

Ali Simon pondered the words of the woman from Cadiz, and she wasn't wrong; with less than half of his servants, he could maintain his mansion.

"You're right, my friend. I know I have too many servants, but I feel good having them around. You know what their fate would be. In a way, I feel good saving them from that uncertain future. Besides, they are my countrymen, people from my land, and I like having them here, hearing them speak with that accent that I recognize and that takes me back to my childhood, Isabel. Perhaps that's the reason. That doesn't mean I'm not losing the money I invested in their purchase. They know they have a debt with me and that to be free, they must settle it."

"I know many slaves end up in the galleys, that there is no escape from that hell, and if they do, they come out battered and scarred for life. In the end, you're doing them a favor, dear Ali. If it weren't for you, many of them wouldn't be in this world."

"My brother Salvador ended his days as a slave on a galley. He never wanted to hear my advice. Once I paid his ransom, but he returned to piracy and was captured again."

"I've heard the story, Ali, but don't forget that each one builds their own path. Your brother followed his. Don't feel responsible."

"Many times I think I could have rescued him, although I know he would have returned to sea and never thanked me."

"Don't torment yourself with that, friend Ali. When do you intend to reply to the bishop?"

"Without delay, Isabel."

"Do you want me to help you draft the letter? I'm good at epistles."

"It's always helpful to have assistance from a lady of high standing, although I'll tell you that since I was seventeen, I've been able to read and write perfectly, not only in Spanish but also in Arabic and Turkish. My adoptive father, El Kaid, insisted that I receive an education. In the Canaries, I never had the opportunity to go to school, and it was something that didn't concern me much, to be honest. You know that the poor are not given any opportunities. However, now I see how important it is to know how to read and write."

"Education is a luxury only a few can afford. But women have it worse; we're only prepared to be good wives and mothers. I learned to read and write because I had a housekeeper who loved reading and spent hours reading endless poems and tales of knights to me."

"You're right, Isabel, education is the privilege of a few, and in the Canaries, it is and remains so. The poorest of the poor have only the right to hunger and misery."

Ali Simon got up and walked to the desk by one of the windows facing south. He sat down, took up the quill, and began to write:

Dear Excellency:

It has pleased me greatly to receive a letter from such an illustrious personality, defender of the Christian faith in the lands where I was born.

I will begin with the last matter as it requires a quicker response. My apostasy from the Christian faith was not a difficult decision. On the contrary, my embrace of Islam has been free, affectionate, and reciprocated.

As for the first matter, which interests me more than the light that feeds my soul, I must tell you that indeed, I have paid for the freedom of most of the Canary slaves I have captured in Barbary and many others from those lands who have requested it. I do so because I too was captured and enslaved, and I was given the opportunity to be free.

As Your Excellency will understand, until they repay the debt they owe me, they cannot leave Algiers. However, while they are here, they are cared for and protected by me. I would have liked to forgive them the debt they still owe me, but it would set a bad example for those of us in the business.

I know you are a man of influence and will take the necessary steps to ensure that the families of the captives can gather, not without effort, the owed amount.

May Allah grant you health and prosperity for many years.

In Algiers, August 20, 1686

When he finished it, he read it over, then went to his friend and said:

"Read it and tell me what you think."

The woman from Cadiz read it carefully and, after a few minutes, said to him:

"It's perfect, Ali. I couldn't have drafted it better. It's evident you've read a lot, and your handwriting is enviable."

"Days at sea afford much time, Isabel. I spend idle hours reading. I came across a trunk full of books from a Spanish ship we captured off the coast of Cadiz. I also practice writing. I have a journal in which I write down the events of the day."

"What a great idea! I imagine you write about me on some pages..."

"Of course, Isabel! I write about a beautiful woman from Cadiz I met in the port of Algiers..."

"For God's sake, Ali, let me read them!"

"No, dear friend, diaries are personal. So you'll have to wait until I die to read them."

"Don't talk about death, Ali! You still have many years and many letters to write in that diary."

"May Allah hear you, my friend. Corsairs are prepared for death. We're playing like children on the edge of a dagger, and we may cut ourselves. When I set sail, I don't know if it will be my last voyage. When we weigh anchor, I remember El Kaid. Who expected him to die on that journey? No one, but a cannon tore through his heart. So since that day, I'm ready to die, and besides, I'm not afraid."

The woman from Cadiz looked into the corsair's eyes and then said to him:

"You have many years ahead of you, dear. You know I'm half a witch, and I see it in your eyes."

"I don't know, Isabel. All I know is that I'm alive and that I have to send this letter to the bishop."

"Let's do it, then, dear Ali."

Ambassador of Algiers

A week after sending the missive, a general from the dey of Algiers' entourage arrived at his mansion and informed him that he had an audience at the palace the following day. The visit caught him off guard while he was having tea with the corsair Chivirino, who happened to be the father of his wife Aminah. Chivirino commented, surprised:

"After being appointed Admiral of the Algerian Navy, what other appointments are awaiting you, Ali?"

"The admiralship of the Algerian Navy was a recognition from our dey for the many benefits I've provided over the years, but it's just a title. Our navy is what it is, you know, four well-equipped ships that depend on the dey. The Turks are the ones who protect us, and they indeed have a powerful navy."

"The admiralty is no ordinary title. Don't downplay its significance, Ali. You are undoubtedly the most prominent corsair in recent years. There hasn't been a corsair or pirate with the progression you've had."

"I had a great teacher and a lot of luck."

"It's true that El Kaid was a great teacher. He taught you the secrets of corsairing, but you've surpassed him. Just look at your feats over the last decade."

Ali Simon thought it was true. He had lost count of the number of ships he had captured and the number of slaves he had taken. He remembered the capture of the Regent of the Audiencia of Seville, which brought the dey 244,000 silver reales and propelled him as one of the most important corsairs in the Mediterranean.

"Flowers overwhelm me, Chivirino."

"Flowers, Ali? Deeds, son. You've earned the fame you have through hard work. That's the reason, and the dey knows it. We all know it."

"I won't deny I've been lucky..."

"Call it what you want, but there are the fruits. There must be a reason why the dey has summoned you."

"Well, I don't know. What's clear is that the dey doesn't summon me for tea. He does it when he needs my services."

"Few have the privilege of earning the dey's favor. And fewer still as a convert."

"Perhaps it has a lot to do with the fact that I'm married to the daughter of a famous Berber who is highly respected in Algiers," Ali said with a smirk.

"Something must have to do with it, ha, ha, ha," he said, smiling. "But you, dear Ali, have earned the respect of those of us who live in this holy city."

"Tomorrow we'll see what news our dear dey brings."

"We'll see. I hope you'll tell me when you have the chance. But with the excitement of the news, I almost forgot the reason for my visit. What are you up to with that Spaniard? My daughter is beside herself. She says you have her as a concubine."

"Those are women's matters, Chivirino. Isabel is a businesswoman, and that's what I discuss with her. I can't deny she's beautiful, and on many occasions, she flirts with me, but we don't go beyond flirting and playing. Don't worry about it. I've told Aminah many times, but she doesn't believe me."

"Don't worry about that; I'll talk to her, and that issue will be closed. I'm not against you taking other wives; I've done it five times myself, but you know my daughter is very jealous."

"I know that. I don't have time for other women; I have enough with her. She satisfies me completely and meets my requirements. She's a good woman."

"Let's not talk anymore, son. The matter is settled. I'll let my daughter know. She'll stop seeing ghosts where there are none."

"I hope she listens to you and closes that door."

"She will, don't worry."

The next morning, Ali rose early, bathed, put on his best clothes, and before the sun was at its zenith, he presented himself before the dey.

He found him seated with two of his ministers discussing the details of constructing a new breakwater in the city's port. Ali waited until one of his chamberlains indicated he was expected.

"Ali! Come closer. Your mission is very important. I want to conclude a mutual defense agreement with the sultan so that, in the event of an attack by any European country, we provide each other with logistical and military assistance. No one knows better than you that we are in the sights of the Spanish, French, English, and Dutch. I've tried to make our city open and cosmopolitan, and indeed we have succeeded, but it's not the first time that, for one reason or another, we have been the target of attacks by some of them."

"And why me, sir?" asked Ali.

"Because you are the perfect representative of the life of this people. We are open-minded individuals who embrace all who live and work for this land. You are a clear example of what I say. You've made yourself, you are the most prominent corsair in my kingdom, and therefore, a high representative of this people."

"Thank you, sir, but perhaps there are others who deserve such distinction."

"Others? Ali, by Allah, you have proven your worth over these years. I won't list the deeds you've performed and the great benefits you've brought to this city and to my reign."

"I am at your service, sir. I will depart when you deem it appropriate. I will strive to be worthy and be a dignified ambassador of your lordship and of Algiers."

"The matter is clear. You will depart the day after tomorrow on a royal galley. You will be accompanied by the highest representatives of my government, and you will deliver this personal letter to the sultan."

Ali Simon took the letter and said to the dey:

"I will strive to rise to the occasion, sir. I hope to be a worthy representative of this country."

"I have no doubt that you will be, Ali."

The corsair returned to his mansion overwhelmed and nervous. He knew that this was the most significant mission ever entrusted to him. He was aware of the importance of relations with Turkey, and on these good relations depended, to a large extent, the immediate future of the corsair city. Turkey was a powerful ally, and the European powers took it into account.

Twenty days later, he returned from his trip to Turkey and was received by the dey in his chambers.

"Ali! What news do you bring? How did it go with Mehmed IV?"

"Good morning, sir. Following your mandate, we concluded a mutual defense agreement in which Turkey guarantees us unconditional support in the event of an attack by any foreign power. I also raised the possibility of closing a trade alliance between the two countries. Sultan Mehmed IV was very interested in further strengthening the trade ties between our nations."

"Magnificent, Ali! That military agreement is essential for our future. Europeans have been considering attacking us as soon as they have the chance. Turkey is our watchdog, ready to bite mercilessly anyone who attacks us. You have been an ambassador who rose to the occasion. I knew I was not mistaken about you."

"Thank you, sir. It has been an honor for me to be Algiers' ambassador. You know I am at your complete disposal."

"I will keep this mission in mind, Ali. I assure you that you will return to Turkey to finalize that trade agreement. Today I will set my scholars to work to prepare the details, and I will write a letter to the sultan expressing my interest in advancing that relationship."

"I reiterate, I am at your full disposal."

"We must celebrate this, Ali. Tomorrow you and your wife will come to dinner. I also extend the invitation to Chivirino. It will be a great feast."

"We will be here, sir."

Ali left the dey's palace satisfied with the work he had done and thought that Algiers was a great country where anyone who worked hard could reach the top, regardless of their origin. He was a clear example. He felt ecstatic. Then, he remembered the days when he was just an apprentice corsair and El Kaid's words predicting he would go far. Yes, he had reached where he never imagined.

The bishop's response

The secretary entered the bishop's office, handed him a letter, and said:

"The letter comes from Algiers. I suppose it's from the renegade, Simón Romero Arráez, Your Excellency."

"If it comes from Algiers, there's no doubt it's his. Let's see what he has to say."

The bishop read the letter carefully and, upon finishing, commented:

"He is not inclined to release any of his captives, nor does he want to follow my advice to return to the fold of the Catholic religion."

"It was to be expected, Your Excellency. You know how renegades are, they only care about the money they can collect, and this is a clear example."

The bishop pondered the words of his secretary and then replied:

"I don't know, Miguel. Something tells me that this renegade, although Islamized, has a Christian soul. The testimonies of the returnees prove it. To the countrymen he captures, he doesn't sell them; instead, he lends them money to buy their freedom and keeps them under his care until they repay their debt. To the Canarian captives in the Baths of Algiers, he also offers to lend them the necessary amount to buy their freedom. I tell you, Miguel, that man is a good Christian, even if he's a confessed Muslim."

"You have a sixth sense, Your Excellency, when it comes to knowing people. You see through them and reach their souls."

"Oh, Miguel! A sixth sense, you say? If I had had that sixth sense, we would never have embarked with that incompetent who didn't know where his right hand was and who led us towards the Americas."

"I don't mean that, Your Excellency. I mean that you have that special gift to know your fellow human beings well, to see what others don't see."

"In the case of Simón Romero, it's not intuition, nor do I rely on any sixth sense; it's just the analysis of the testimonies of Christians who have been captive in Algiers. Those testimonies tell me that this Christian has Islamized because circumstances forced him to. He's a clever man and has only adapted to the reality he lives in. As Jesus Christ said: 'By their fruits ye shall know them,' and the facts speak for themselves, Miguel. Simón Romero, in some way, is helping his countrymen for a reason I don't know."

"The reason is nothing but usury, Your Excellency. He lends them money only to later charge them the corresponding interest."

"No, Miguel. We have evidence that he doesn't charge them interest. He lends them the money and only expects them to pay it back. His desire is not to become rich because he already is. I believe he only wants to help his neighbor, and that is very Christian. We must insist. I will write him another letter to see if I can open the Christian heart he undoubtedly has. Leave me; I am going to draft a letter. Order that lunch be prepared for me and do not forget that the soft-boiled eggs must be just right."

"I will do as you say, Your Excellency."

When the prelate was alone in his office, he began to write the letter.

Dear Simón:

I hope that upon the arrival of this letter, you and your family are in good health.

I suppose you have carefully studied the possibilities for freeing the captives who are under your protection and guardianship. I must tell you that here, the situation is so dire that there is no currency for redemption mainly because the English have stopped importing the fine Malvasia wine grown in the Islands. Even the hardworking vine growers have stopped cultivating their vines because they do not find good business in it.

The economic crisis has reached such a point that these good Christians and people of God have stopped paying tithes to the Holy Mother Church. There are some unfortunate souls whose lands and animals have been seized for non-payment of debts.

With this, I want to expose to you the painful situation of the economy in the Islands so that you can get a real idea of the particular circumstances of the relatives of the captives, who cannot afford to pay for their freedom.

To these poor Christian souls forgotten by God, there is no alternative but to hope that your good heart will take pity on them and not condemn them to die of hunger in the Algerian dungeons for failing to pay their debts.

I beg you to delve into the Christian soul that undoubtedly you possess and act with charity towards your countrymen, who have committed no other crime than leaving the Islands to seek sustenance for their families.

Finally, I reiterate that you return to the path of God the Father because He never forgets and shelters His wayward sheep.

God keep you and yours.

Gran Canaria, October 28, 1686

He called his secretary and ordered him to send the letter.

The redemption

Francisco entered Ali Simon's office and asked, "May I come in, sir?"

"Come in, Francisco. What's the matter?" Ali said, gesturing for him to enter.

"Another letter has arrived from the Bishop of the Canaries," the servant said, handing the corsair the letter.

"Thank you, Francisco."

Ali broke the seal of the envelope, took out the letter, and read it. Upon finishing, he pondered the issues raised by the bishop and knew, from direct information coming from the Islands, that the economic situation was becoming increasingly dire, and the captives would find it very difficult to repay their debts.

He made a list of the captives under his custody. Counting them, there were six. He noted the amount for their liberation and then made the corresponding sum. It was a considerable sum.

Without delay, he sat down and replied to the bishop:

"Your Excellency,

It is a pleasure to receive another missive from you. I am aware that the situation in the Canaries is complex, and many of my countrymen are suffering economic hardships. So much so, that it will be nearly impossible for me to obtain payment for the debts of my captives. I have carefully studied the issue you raise and the potential repercussions of such a decision. Nevertheless, knowing the losses that the liberation of my six captives will incur, I have decided to comply with your request, adhering to the principle of charity that good Muslims must profess.

I am aware that a redemption organized by the Trinitarian monks is scheduled in the coming weeks. I hereby inform you that I will forgive the debts of the six Canarian captives under my custody, and they may return safely to their place of residence.

May Allah grant you health and prosperity for many years.

In Algiers, 1st December 1686

Ali Simon felt a great inner satisfaction as he sealed the letter and sent it to the bishop. He knew it would be years before his captives could repay their debts to him, but he wanted to show indulgence to his fellow countrymen. Behind this gesture would come many others, as Ali Simon continued to lend money so that his captives, Canarians or not, could buy their freedom and thus avoid being sold to the highest bidder in the slave market of Algiers.

***

A week later, Francisco, one of the servants listed for release, knocked on his office door. The corsair responded, "Come in, Francisco, tell me."

"I just wanted to let you know that the Turk Suleiman has sent you a message."

"The Turk Suleiman?"

"Yes, he says there's a captive in the Baths of Algiers asking for you. He says he's your brother and his name is Gaspar."

"Gaspar? I have a brother by that name, but the last I heard, he was in the Americas."

"Do you want me to find out more at the Baths, sir? I'll go down, gather information, and then tell you the details."

"No, Francisco, prepare the carriage and accompany me. We leave immediately."

"How long has it been since I saw my brother Gaspar?" he wondered. More than thirty years. Gaspar was the eldest of his siblings and had left to seek fortune in America at the first opportunity. He remembered that when he embarked for Cabo Bojador, Gaspar had been gone for over three years. They knew of him because he sent a letter each year, telling them about his life in that continent of endless discovery.

As he dressed, he thought about his older brother. He nostalgically recalled the days when they went fishing in their parents' boat. They would set out at dawn and sail two miles out to sea. His brother Gaspar used to say it was the best time because the fish were still asleep, not able to see clearly, they would eat the bait without looking and swallow the hook down to their gills.

When he arrived at the Baths of Algiers, the activity was frenetic. Captives of various nationalities entered and exited. Before stepping down from the carriage, he perceived that scent, a mixture of sweat, urine, and excrement emanating from the overcrowded cells of men, women, and children. Captors tried to sell the slaves as quickly as possible because they knew that an extended stay in the Baths could mean losing more than half due to illness. Infectious diseases spread too easily in those filthy cells where hygiene was nonexistent.

He entered and asked the military officer in charge of the Baths for Gaspar Romero Arráez. The officer recognized him, greeted him, and searched for the name in the records he kept in a folder made of tanned camel leather. After a while, he found it and said:

"Yes, here it is. He's accompanied by his wife and a fifteen-year-old son. The captives belong to the corsair Suleiman. There he is. Talk to him. He's a good Muslim. You won't have any problems reaching an agreement."

Ali Simon was more than accustomed to negotiating with the corsairs and pirates to whom he sold and bought slaves, and on occasion, he had done business with Suleiman. He made his way through the captives and reached the place where the corsair was. He was sitting, counting coins and putting them into a leather bag. He was a sun-browned man, stout, with a beard and mustache, and he wore a blue turban that covered most of his face.

"Assalamu Alaykum, Suleiman," Alí Simon said.

"Wa Alaykum Assalām, Ali. Long time no see in these parts! I heard that you were in Turkey representing our dear pasha and that you've been appointed admiral of the Algerian fleet. You've done well since the great El Kaid passed away. You had the best teacher. The greatest corsair to ever set foot in this holy land."

"Yes, I've done well, but you know it's only the result of hard work, some luck, and, most importantly, having had El Kaid as a mentor. He taught me everything I know."

"You were his most promising student, and he loved you like a son."

"Yes, I know, and I also considered him a father."

"How can I help you, Ali?"

"You have a Christian captive who might be my brother."

"Your brother? Isn't he the one you freed from the galleys a few years ago?"

Ali remembered his brother Salvador and felt saddened. It had been many years since he had heard anything about him, and he was likely dead.

"No, it's my older brother. The name and surnames match. His wife and son are also with him."

"Let me see, tell me his name, Ali."

"Gaspar Romero Arráez."

"Of course, it's him! I remember. Since we captured him, he hasn't stopped insisting that he's your brother, and just yesterday, I sent you a personal message about it. Wait, I'll have him brought here."

The corsair called one of his men. He ordered him to find the captive and, if he was there, to bring him along with his wife and son.

"If it's him, I imagine you'll buy his freedom and that of his family, but you know the boy will cost you double."

"Yes, I know, don't worry about that. I'll pay whatever you ask, Suleiman. I won't haggle over a single gold coin if it's for my brother."

"Oh, blood, how it pulls! For it, we are willing to give our all."

"You would do the same."

"I don't know. I have no brothers or close relatives. They died from the Black Death. I am the last of my line, and with me, it will disappear."

A disheveled man approached, walking with his head down. He had a beard of over three weeks. Ali Simon observed him carefully but didn't recognize him. It had been many, many years. His brother left when he was nearly twenty-five, and it had been over thirty since he last saw him. The Canary approached, lifted the man's head, and recognized him. It was Gaspar. However, his brother didn't recognize him at first until Ali Simon said:

"I'm your brother Simon, Gaspar."

Gaspar lifted his head, opened his eyes as if seeing a ghostly specter, and said in a sorrowful voice:

"The Lord Jesus Christ has heard my prayers. Thank God it's you, brother. Thank God you've come to rescue me. I don't know what would have become of us, Simon."

He embraced his brother, and tears welled up in his eyes.

"You're safe, you and your family."

"Thank you, Simon, thank you! I thought I would never leave here, and I feared for my wife, but above all for my son, who is also named Simon. I baptized him with your name when I heard you had become a Muslim."

"I still keep my name, Gaspar. They know me as Ali Simon, Ali Romero, or Ali the Canary. However, that doesn't matter. Wait here; I'll sort out the matter of the ransom payment."

"I'll pay you every last coin you spend on me and my family."

The corsair looked at him, smiled, and said:

"Don't worry about that, Gaspar. Money is not a problem for me. So, as I said, wait here."

Ali Simon finalized the payment with Suleiman and took his brother to his palace. He instructed his servants to prepare the guest room and bath and to set everything for lunch because he assumed his brother and his family hadn't eaten anything decent in the past week.

Lunch was served in the main hall of Ali Simon's palace. Gaspar entered, feeling shy, enjoying the beauty of his brother's palace, which had been built in white limestone with many Moorish arches on doors and windows, giving incredible luminosity to all the rooms of the building.

When they were seated, the corsair made the proper introductions:

"This is my wife, Aminah, and my sons, El Kaid, Ali Juan, and my daughter Adila. El Kaid is the eldest, almost twenty years old, Ali Juan, sixteen, and Adila, thirteen."

"She is Juana María, my wife, and he is Simón, who is the same age as your daughter and, as I told you, he's named after you," said his brother Gaspar.

"It's an honor," the corsair said, smiling.

"You know, when we were children, we got along very well. You were my favorite brother because Salvador was very much to himself. By the way, do you know what happened to him? The last I heard, our father told me he had embarked to become a corsair."

Ali Simon thought about whether it was convenient to tell his brother the truth and decided that he would, although he would leave out the last part.

"Yes, what our father told you is true, but they captured him, and I had to pay for his freedom. I offered him some money to stop being a corsair and help our parents. He didn't like my offer and went back to sea. They captured him again, and the last I heard of him was that he was assigned to the galleys."

"To the galleys?"

"Yes, Gaspar."

"How long ago was that, Simon?"

"Two or three years. I don't remember exactly."

"If that's the case, our brother has probably perished. I've been told that being assigned to the galleys is the worst fate; once you're in, you never get out."

"That's true, but Salvador was consumed by greed, envy, and pride. He wanted to become a famous corsair..."

"Like you?"

"I've only been lucky. I learned a lot when I was young alongside the greatest corsair who ever lived in Algiers. After that, I just went along with the circumstances of life, doing what I had to do at each moment. Salvador made a mistake and paid dearly for it."

"Not all of us have your good fortune, Simon. From a young age, it was clear you were a clever and brave boy. Others have tried as hard, but in the end, we haven't succeeded," he said sadly.

"I suppose you were coming from the Americas when they captured you."

"Yes, they attacked us a few miles from Gran Canaria when we could see it with the naked eye. However, the pirates boarded us and captured us."

"Things didn't go well for you in America?"

"No, Simon. I couldn't realize the project I had in mind. I wanted to be a baker, but when you get there, you realize there's much to do, and you need a lot of money to prosper. Supporting a family becomes nearly impossible."

"What do you want to do in the Canaries?"

"I don't know. I'll return with nothing because the money I had managed to save has been stolen from me. It wasn't much, but enough to start some business in Las Palmas."

"I could give you a loan with the condition that, instead of paying me back, you pay our parents. They need it, and I know father isn't working."

Gaspar thought about the offer his brother was making.

"It would be good and a way to help our parents, but I'll also have to pay you back for what you've spent on us."

"When did you get married, Gaspar?"

His brother looked at him puzzled, not understanding why he was asking about his wedding when they were talking about money matters.

"I got married... fifteen years ago," he hesitated for a moment.

"Fifteen years and ten months," his wife added.

"And you didn't invite me to the wedding?"

His brother didn't understand why Ali Simon was so concerned about his wedding. He thought maybe old age was affecting him or he was losing his mind.

"I would have loved for you to attend. Not only you, but also our family. It was a very intimate wedding, just the two witnesses and the priest."

"Then I didn't give you my wedding gift, so my gift will be the amount I paid for your freedom and that of your family."

"That's a lot of money, Simon."

"Don't worry about it, Gaspar. Money is not a problem for me. So, as I said, that's the deal. Are you in agreement?"

Gaspar stood up, walked over to where his brother was, and said:

"Of course I agree, Simon. Give me a hug."

Ali Simon stood up and hugged his brother.

"I'll never forget what you've done for my family. The day we were captured, I thought my life was over, and when I learned we were in Algiers, a window of hope opened, although I didn't know if you were alive or dead, Simon. I know many don't approve of you being a corsair and wish you dead, but deep down, I know you're a good person. A bad person wouldn't do what you've done for my family."

"I don't care what others think, Gaspar. I engage in corsairing because I don't know how to do anything else, and besides, I'm good at it. Many times I've thought about returning, but at this point in my life, I want to die here. In a sense, I'm a part of this place, and if we tally it up, I've spent many more years in Algiers than in the Canaries."

"I don't reproach you for anything, brother. I just want to thank you. Remember that I am in your debt."

"Gaspar, now you need to rest and recover. In a week, a redemption is scheduled, and a ship will come to take you to Gran Canaria."

"What's a redemption?"

"If the relatives of some captives manage to raise enough money to pay for their freedom, three or four times a year, those relatives send a ship with a safe-conduct from Algiers that prevents it from being attacked. Generally, it's the Trinitarian monks who handle redemptions."

"Will we leave on that ship?"

"Yes. Don't worry. I'll make sure of it. Rest and recover."

"Thank you, Simon."

"There's nothing to thank, you're my brother. I'm convinced you would do the same for me, Gaspar. As I said, rest."

***

The Corsair had planned for his servant, Francisco, to accompany his brother to Gran Canaria along with the six captives he had decided to set free. This would fulfill the commitment he had made to Bishop Bartolomé García Ximénez de Rabadán. A week before departure, Ali Simon notified him of his impending release. He called him to his office and said:

"Francisco, you have served me faithfully over these years. Next week, you will leave on the Trinitarian monks' ship. Your debt has been settled. In a week's time, you will be a free man as you once were."

"Thank you, sir, but I would like to remain in your service."

"What do you mean, Francisco? Why do you want to stay here? I'm giving you the opportunity to return to your family."

"I know, sir, and I'm very grateful. Please, use my spot for another captive. There are some whose families eagerly await them."

"And you, Francisco? What about you and your family?"

"No one is waiting for me in the Canaries, sir. I am an only child, and my parents passed away years ago. There, only misery and hunger await me. I know the economic situation in the Islands is not the best in these times, and I also know that finding decent work to make a living is very difficult, if not impossible."

"As you wish, Francisco, you will continue in my service, but with one condition."

"Tell me, sir?"

"That you accept wages for your work. Remember, you are a free man, and free men, when they work, must receive something in return."

"I already feel well paid with the accommodation and food you provide me. That is payment enough."

"No, Francisco, that payment is not enough. Trust me on this; I won't argue further."

"I want to tell you something I've never told you before."

"What do you want to tell me?"

"Thanks to you, I am still alive. I am a man of almost fifty-five years, and my fate would have been nothing but the galleys, where I would have undoubtedly died. You rescued me from the Baths of Algiers without asking for anything in return, and I will be eternally grateful. I do not know why you did it, nor am I interested. The truth is, you gave me the chance to keep on living. I heard your brother say that you were a good man, and it's true, you are. Not just my opinion."

"Others do not think the same, Francisco. If you think about it, I am not such a good man. I raid ships, and until recently, I raided entire towns, enslaving captives to sell to the highest bidder. That doesn't make one a good Muslim or a good Christian. So don't say I'm a good man," he said with a tone of sadness and reproach.

Francisco knew he had a point. Seen in that light, Ali Simon was a man without scruples who engaged in piracy to enrich himself, regardless of the harm it might cause his fellow man.

"If I'm not a good man, why do I lend money to the captives of the Islands, why do I grant freedom to you without asking for anything in return, why am I going to set free six of my servants, even though they haven't repaid the loan I granted them? Why did I help your father, your brother Salvador, and now I'm doing it with your brother Gaspar?"

"To try to cleanse my conscience, Francisco. Because I know what I'm doing is not right, even though I couldn't do anything else to earn a living. I am a corsair, and we should not have a conscience. Leave me, I want to rest. Remember what I told you."

"Thank you, sir."

***

Exactly two weeks later, his brother Gaspar and his family would depart for Gran Canaria with the five captives the corsair had set free. The vessel they were scheduled to depart on had been chartered by the Trinitarian monks, who had been undertaking this redemptive work for many years and would continue to do so for many more, with varying degrees of success.

Ali Simon accompanied his brother and his family to the port of Algiers. Once there, the Berber corsair said to his brother:

"Don't forget our deal, Gaspar. Our parents need you. I can't send them money because it would be confiscated. The inquisitors know who I am and control any money I might send to the Canaries. So, when you arrive, be discreet, Gaspar, so that your business can thrive and no one suspects it has been financed with money from piracy."

"Don't worry, I'll be discreet and take care of our parents until the end of their days. I promise you."

Ali Simon hugged his brother and nephew, nodded to his sister-in-law, and bid them farewell.

He waited until the three-masted ship unfurled its sails and set off towards Gran Canaria.

He would have liked to go on that ship, to accompany his elder brother and return so that his life could be like it was in his childhood years. However, he knew there was no turning back.

He watched as the ship disappeared into the horizon until it was out of sight. Then, Francisco asked him:

"Shall we go, sir?"

"Yes, Francisco, let's go."

"Do you miss our homeland?"

"Yes, I miss the memories, which are fading more and more. You know what they say, things are not as they are, but as they are remembered. Come on, let's go, I have many things to do."

They vanished into the streets of Algiers. Ali Simon pondered what would have become of him if he had stayed in Gran Canaria, what would have become of his life if he had never boarded the fishing boat Las Ánimas, if he had never met El Kaid, and if he had not turned to piracy. He longed for his homeland and its people, but he knew he wouldn't trade his life for any other. He was happy.

The hardest apprenticeship

Ali Simon, with almost fifty years, worried that his son showed no interest in becoming a corsair. He had ventured out one or two times with his men on raids in the Mediterranean. The canary allowed him to do so because he wanted his son to experience being a sailor and a corsair so that he would eventually make up his mind.

The truth was, his son showed enthusiasm, and the references from his trusted men were good. They said he was an excellent sailor with great potential to become a good corsair.

One afternoon, Ali Simon called him into his office and said, "I know you want to become a corsair, my son, but you know I have three ships that are on the commercial route with Turkey, and I need a man to take charge of that business. Who better than my own son? You know that no one cares for the chickens better than their owner."

"I know, father, but I have already embarked several times and enjoyed it like never before."

"Yes, son, but you know that being a corsair carries risks, and those risks can cost you your life."

"Why don't you want me to pursue something you dedicated yourself to? Are you afraid I'll surpass you? That I'll be a better corsair than you?"

"No, son, I don't fear that. I only fear that you embark and never return. That is my only fear. Remember that arrogance and complacency are bad traveling companions. I only tell you that you have the opportunity to do something different and safer. I didn't have that opportunity, and if I had, I would have taken it without hesitation. I've seen many of my men die to know that corsair life is no child's play."

"Sorry, father, I let myself be carried away by enthusiasm, but I want to try, and I want to do it with you, for you to teach me what you know and reveal your secrets. If it turns out that I'm not cut out for corsair life, I promise I'll take care of the commercial ship business."

Ali Simon knew his son was a magnificent sailor and, therefore, would be an extraordinary corsair. There was no doubt he had it in his blood, and if that were the case, it would be very difficult to change his mind. You couldn't go against nature. His son El Kaid was born to be a corsair.

Having seen what he saw, he decided to make his last trip as a Berber corsair accompanied by his son El Kaid. After that trip, he had decided to fully dedicate himself to his nascent commercial activity.

They embarked on one of his newly built ships to teach him the secrets of corsair life. He knew that the slave trade was still a big business with great future prospects, but it was an activity not without many and dangerous risks.

Ali Simon knew that corsairs and pirates dominated most of the Mediterranean and much of the South Atlantic, territories where they continued to raid ships and, on rare occasions, make incursions into coastal towns.

The corsair chose the crew; he wanted to take the most competent ones with him. He didn't want to take unnecessary risks, and the best way to do that was to have the best.

They set sail at dawn. Ali Simon knew his son had much to learn, and the only way for him to do so was by sailing. The corsair realized that his son easily grasped maritime concepts and made them his own immediately. The reports that his son was a good sailor were not far from reality at all.

What kept the corsair awake at night was El Kaid's safety. This time it wasn't about him but about his son, and putting him at risk was a matter of concern. He was flesh of his flesh.

After a few days of sailing, they approached the shores of Cape Bojador and made some raids, capturing some fishing boats with their respective crews. Ali Simon said to his son, "After a month and a half of sailing, I think we should set course for Algiers. As an experience, it's quite good. You've learned to handle a ship without anyone's help, and you do it almost perfectly. We've captured two vessels and have thirty slaves to sell in the market. What more could we ask for? Next time, you will come alone and will be in command."

"Father, with all due respect, I believe we should continue until we capture a big ship, a galley, a galleon, or a brig like the one you told me you boarded off the coast of Portugal and with which you earned a lot of money and fame. Coming into port with this meager booty would ruin our reputation."

"My son, you will have time to reach for better spoils. Prestige is gained over the years and with much wisdom. I've told you about your uncle Salvador, who wanted to conquer the world in three days and ended up on a French galley. Take the good from this experience, what you've learned, and what you can apply when you're alone at sea. Now it's time to return, son, and that's not up for discussion. You also need to learn to obey the orders of your superiors. Here, on this deck, I am not your father, El Kaid," he said, cutting the conversation short.

The son went to his cabin with a pout of anger, maintaining the respect and silence his father had taught him.

The canary knew his son had much to learn. His youth and impulsiveness led him to lose sight of reality. In a way, he reminded him of himself when he was young, and he remembered the moment when he was captured by the old corsair El Kaid. He smiled, recalling that action that could have cost him his life if his second father hadn't intervened. The corsair saw in him what no one else had seen in a moment of passing madness; he saw an act of bravery.

***

At dawn, the cries of the lookout awakened him:

"A galleon to port! A galleon to port!"

Ali Simon jumped out of bed, dressed as quickly as he could, and rushed up on deck. Upon arrival, his son was giving orders to steer the bow towards the galleon.

"What are you doing, El Kaid?" he asked, indignant.

"Going after that galleon, that's a worthy prey for a pirate like you and your firstborn."

"You still have much to learn," he said, pulling him away from the helm.

"But, father, what are you doing?" he asked, not understanding.

"Tell me. How many cannons does it have on the port side? Answer me!" he shouted while veering in the opposite direction of the Spanish ship.

"One, two, three, four, five. Twenty, father, it has twenty," he answered with a shout.

"Sir, they've aimed the bow at us!" shouted the lookout from the mast.

"It's a Spanish galleon, and if it has twenty cannons on each side, they're among the latest ones built. They're destructive and very effective because they've already sunk several Barbary ships and they have the mission to protect the fleet coming and going from the Americas. May Allah protect us, son, may Allah protect us."

The first impact was heard about twenty meters from the bow of the Barbary ship. Ali Simon realized that the fishing boats trailing behind were a burden, so he shouted:

"Cut the cables of the fishing boats, they're acting as ballast and hindering maneuvers, damn it!"

El Kaid jumped towards the stern like a bat out of hell, with his saber in hand, and cut the cables tying the boats at the stern.

The cannon shots became more frequent, and the impacts much closer. Meanwhile, the Barbary ship kept veering back and forth to escape the blazing projectiles of the galleon.

El Kaid said to his father:

"They're unfurling all sails, father."

"I see it. It will be very complicated to escape their cannon shots, we're not as fast and they have twenty cannons firing at us non-stop. They know they're superior and won't let us escape."

"We'll surely escape, father!"

As the Spanish ship unfurled its sails, its speed increased, and it began to glide over the sea. Ali continued with the escape maneuvers, although he saw the enemy ship's bow getting closer and closer, until a cannon shot destroyed the starboard bow. Ali veered again, but the projectiles fell on either side of the vessel, to the bow, stern, port, and starboard, until one split the main mast in two.

Ali Simon saw the sail fall and understood that his adventure had come to an end, that they would be destroyed by cannon shots until not a trace of their ship remained, lost in the depths of the Atlantic.

"Abandon ship, you'll be safer in the water. Everyone out, into the water!" he shouted, desperate.

His men jumped into the water. Most perished drowning because they couldn't swim. The luckier ones managed to stay afloat by clinging to the remains of the Barbary corsair's ship.

Ali Simon still clung to the helm with the firm determination to go down with his ship, watching as the projectiles fell on either side, destroying his vessel. Then, his son grabbed him by the arm and forced him to jump overboard.

Clutching onto a piece of the mast, the Barbary and his son watched as the sea swallowed the vessel in a matter of minutes. A bleak future lay ahead of them.

From the water, they observed a boat approaching, picking up survivors who weren't badly injured and finishing off those who weren't useful, to be sold as slaves or to work in the galleys. When the boat reached the father and son, one of the rescued fishermen shouted:

At dawn, the cries of the lookout awakened him:

"A galleon to port! A galleon to port!"

Ali Simon jumped out of bed, dressed as quickly as he could, and rushed up on deck. Upon arrival, his son was giving orders to steer the bow towards the galleon.

"What are you doing, El Kaid?" he asked, indignant.

"Going after that galleon, that's a worthy prey for a pirate like you and your firstborn."

"You still have much to learn," he said, pulling him away from the helm.

"But, father, what are you doing?" he asked, not understanding.

"Tell me. How many cannons does it have on the port side? Answer me!" he shouted while veering in the opposite direction of the Spanish ship.

"One, two, three, four, five. Twenty, father, it has twenty," he answered with a shout.

"Sir, they've aimed the bow at us!" shouted the lookout from the mast.

"It's a Spanish galleon, and if it has twenty cannons on each side, they're among the latest ones built. They're destructive and very effective because they've already sunk several Barbary ships and they have the mission to protect the fleet coming and going from the Americas. May Allah protect us, son, may Allah protect us."

The first impact was heard about twenty meters from the bow of the Barbary ship. Ali Simon realized that the fishing boats trailing behind were a burden, so he shouted:

"Cut the cables of the fishing boats, they're acting as ballast and hindering maneuvers, damn it!"

El Kaid jumped towards the stern like a bat out of hell, with his saber in hand, and cut the cables tying the boats at the stern.

The cannon shots became more frequent, and the impacts much closer. Meanwhile, the Barbary ship kept veering back and forth to escape the blazing projectiles of the galleon.

El Kaid said to his father:

"They're unfurling all sails, father."

"I see it. It will be very complicated to escape their cannon shots, we're not as fast and they have twenty cannons firing at us non-stop. They know they're superior and won't let us escape."

"We'll surely escape, father!"

As the Spanish ship unfurled its sails, its speed increased, and it began to glide over the sea. Ali continued with the escape maneuvers, although he saw the enemy ship's bow getting closer and closer, until a cannon shot destroyed the starboard bow. Ali veered again, but the projectiles fell on either side of the vessel, to the bow, stern, port, and starboard, until one split the main mast in two.

Ali Simon saw the sail fall and understood that his adventure had come to an end, that they would be destroyed by cannon shots until not a trace of their ship remained, lost in the depths of the Atlantic.

"Abandon ship, you'll be safer in the water. Everyone out, into the water!" he shouted, desperate.

His men jumped into the water. Most perished drowning because they couldn't swim. The luckier ones managed to stay afloat by clinging to the remains of the Barbary corsair's ship.

Ali Simon still clung to the helm with the firm determination to go down with his ship, watching as the projectiles fell on either side, destroying his vessel. Then, his son grabbed him by the arm and forced him to jump overboard.

Clutching onto a piece of the mast, the Barbary and his son watched as the sea swallowed the vessel in a matter of minutes. A bleak future lay ahead of them.

From the water, they observed a boat approaching, picking up survivors who weren't badly injured and finishing off those who weren't useful, to be sold as slaves or to work in the galleys. When the boat reached the father and son, one of the rescued fishermen shouted:

"That's the captain of the pirates! Cut the throat of that Moorish dog who is also a damned renegade."

One of the sailors on the galleon raised his saber to kill the two pirates, but Ali Simon intervened and said in perfect Spanish:

"I am Ali Simon, consul of the dey of Algiers."

"You're an infidel dog who will be food for the sharks," replied the sailor.

"Before they execute me, I demand to speak with the person in charge of this ship. Then you can throw me overboard or cut my throat. Besides, I'm a valuable prize, you can always exchange me for a good number of captives or collect a juicy ransom," the renegade replied calmly.

The sailor analyzed the words of the corsair and thought he had a point; he was a valuable catch, so he lowered his saber and said:

"Alright. Christian charity and your Moorish title will prolong your life, but only until we verify if what you say is true. If not, you'll end up in a damned bonfire, devilish Moor. Get them on board!"

After a few minutes, they were on the deck of the galleon, chained, soaked, and shivering with cold.

Ali Simon knew that the chances of survival were slim. He knew that pirates were executed or, in the best cases, condemned to the galleys, although he had a glimmer of hope being a person of high rank in Algiers.

The captain of the galleon approached where the prisoners were. He walked around them two or three times and asked:

"Who do you say you are?" he asked, looking at him arrogantly.

"I am Ali Simon Romero Arráez, consul of the dey of Algiers."

"Ah, Ali Simon, The Canary, the famous corsair and bastard renegade. Yes, we've heard of you. And you say you're the consul of that den of thieves that is Algiers?"

"Yes, I am the consul of the dey of Algiers."

With the cane he held in his right hand, he struck him across the face. The blow knocked him down, and he shouted:

"You are nothing! You are a wretch who will be judged and burned on the largest pyre as a renegade and infidel. Besides, the Kingdom of Spain does not recognize those infidel Moors who live off theft and slavery."

His son made a gesture to respond to the aggression and received another blow that marked his face from side to side. The Barbary rose slowly to catch his breath. He felt his feet trembling and his face burning. He had never been hit with such fury and rage. When he was on his feet, Ali helped his son up. With his gaze, he told him to let it be and then addressed the captain:

"You know as well as I do that for the Kingdom of Spain, I have a price, so I recommend you stop using gratuitous violence, direct your ship to the nearest port, and put me at the disposal of the authorities."

"I could also throw you overboard, and the sharks would have a great feast with your infidel dog meat, and no one would know. You're worth nothing and nobody. From now on, you're just an infidel who deserves no respect."

"I repeat," he said, raising his voice so that the whole crew could hear him, "I am Ali Simon Romero Arráez, consul of the dey of Algiers and general of the Algerian Navy."

"We've heard you. Conversation's over. In a week, we'll be in the port of Gran Canaria for you to be judged by the Tribunal of the Holy Inquisition. They will decide what to do with you."

"What Allah decrees, I will accept willingly."

The captain struck him again with such force that Ali Simon fell forward, nearly losing consciousness. This time, the blow landed directly on his right temple. He felt a pain he could barely bear. Gritting his teeth, he managed to struggle to his feet with great difficulty, thanks to his son's help. His sense of balance was lost, and his vision completely blurred.

"Accursed renegade! If I could, I'd execute you right here. You're saved because many good Christians are rotting in the prisons of

Algiers, and you or your lackeys could be used as bargaining chips for their release. Take them below and keep them on bread and water during the journey. These are traitors and enemies, and they must be treated as such. Show no mercy! They've never shown any to the Christians they've captured in good faith. We must repay them in kind."

They were lowered into the hold and locked in a compartment that served as a cell. When they were alone, Ali Simon asked his son:

"How are you feeling?"

"Fine, father, fine," he said, crestfallen. "How are you feeling? That scoundrel gave you two good blows."

"I'm alright, somewhat sore, but alright. I still have some strength left."

"It's my fault we're here. If I hadn't insisted on you coming with me, you'd be safe in Algiers. If I had listened to you and taken charge of our three merchant ships..."

"Don't torment yourself with that, son. They knew we were corsairs. Remember, we had three fishing boats trailing behind us. That warship would have come after us, and sooner or later, it would have caught up with us. We might have had a chance if we had spotted it far in advance and hadn't had it so close, but that wasn't the case. We have to focus our efforts on surviving. We're valuable pieces, and they can trade us or even ransom us."

"I'm the one to blame for this situation, father," El Kaid said again, ignoring his father. "If I hadn't insisted on you accompanying me, you'd be safe in Algiers. If I had listened to you and taken charge of our three merchant ships..."

"I'm here because I wanted to be, no one forced me. I've been sailing for many years, and I know perfectly well the risks of being a pirate, and this is one of them. You have to understand that every time we set sail, our lives are at risk. That's the life of a corsair, always hanging by a thread. I've told you once, the best corsair I ever knew, El Kaid, died in battle. If we survive this, which I hope we do, you have to appreciate what you have at your disposal. Risks must be taken when there's no other way out, when there's no other path to follow. I became a corsair because I had no other choice. It was the only way I could make a living. You, son, have new possibilities ahead of you. Don't hesitate to seize them. You have to learn from this situation."

"Nevertheless, father, I would like to be a corsair, to sail and carve out my own future like you did."

"Perhaps our capture is a sign from Allah. If after this, you still want to be a corsair, I won't stop you, son, but you don't need to be a corsair; others have no other way out. So reflect, analyze what you have in your favor and what you have against you. You're going to have time, plenty of time to think."

"Thank you, father. The only good thing about being here is that you're with me, and that gives me strength to endure the ordeal that lies ahead."

"Resist, son, resist, we have no other way out. Grit your teeth and move forward."

The galleon dropped anchor in the anchorage of Bahía de Las Isletas. As Ali Simon climbed on deck, he breathed the air of the land he had left over thirty-two years ago to fish off the coast of Cape Bojador. He recognized the beaches, the mountains, and the city; little had changed. He looked at his son and said with tears in his eyes:

"Your father was born here. In this land of noble and grateful people."

"And perhaps we won't leave here again, father," his son said pessimistically.

"That remains to be seen. Luckily, your father, my son, has sown in the soul of this land, and perhaps we will see the fruits. Allah protects us."

A sailor interrupted their conversation with the sound of a whip cracking on the deck and said to them:

"Less chatter and more walking; you're going to spend a few weeks in the most welcoming place in Gran Canaria."

After the boat reached land, Ali Simon and his son El Kaid were led to the dungeons of the fortress of Castillo de Mata, and the members of their crew were sold as slaves to the highest bidder.

Bishop and lawyer

Bishop Bartolomé García Ximénez Rabadán was in permanent rest on the island of Tenerife when his secretary entered his office and said:

"Good morning, Your Eminence."

"Good morning, Miguel. What's so important that it interrupts my writing?"

"I know, sir, that you've instructed me to only disturb you with matters of utmost importance, and I believe this qualifies."

"What is it, Miguel?" he asked, somewhat annoyed.

"It's regarding an Inquisition trial, Your Eminence."

"By God, Miguel, I've given orders for those matters to be handled at the episcopal seat, and when necessary, I draft the corresponding report for the tribunal. I suppose this matter is different. Tell me, you have me intrigued."

The secretary approached the bishop solemnly and said:

"It concerns Simón Romero, Alí Romero. Do you remember, Your Eminence? The renegade."

The prelate recalled the exchange of letters and the freeing of captives a few years prior.

"Of course I remember, Miguel, how could I forget? I may be old and sick, but my memory is intact. What's happened to him?"

"He was captured off the coast of Barbary and will be judged by the Holy Tribunal. I fear that, unless something changes, he will be condemned to the stake."

The bishop knew the Inquisition would show no mercy to the convert and would condemn him outright to burning.

"What are we to do, Miguel?" he asked almost to himself.

"I don't know. I just wanted you to know. Perhaps you would like to write a report in favor of the corsair because we know he aided many of his countrymen and freed a few through his mediation. Maybe the tribunal will take your words into consideration and spare him the inevitable."

The bishop quickly analyzed his secretary's words and said:

"That report won't make a difference. I know the members of the Holy Tribunal very well, and I know my words will fall on deaf ears."

"You lose nothing by trying, Your Eminence. I know you hold that renegade in high esteem."

"Yes, Miguel, you're right, I do. I believe the only way to help him will be to go in person to try to mitigate the sentence, at least to spare him from the death he's destined for."

"Do you think such a journey is necessary? Remember our experiences with ships have been, in most cases, disastrous. I fear to set sail again."

"I know, Miguel. We'll entrust ourselves to God the Father, but remember, we've emerged victorious from the assaults of the sea if I recall correctly. We came out unscathed from our first voyage, barely, and also from the storm in the Caribbean when we left Puerto Rico, remember?"

"How could I forget, Your Eminence!"

"And the storm that accompanied us when we made the first pastoral visit to the island of La Palma and the one that hit us when we went to see our episcopal seat in Gran Canaria for the first time and ended up on the other side of the island. Our relationship with the sea has been rather peculiar, and it won't be now that we back down when this supposed infidel needs us."

"And don't forget the storm that accompanied us when we went to make your pastoral visit to the island of Fuerteventura."

"True, Miguel. I had forgotten about that one. Age, my old friend, takes its toll on memory. Remember that in a few days it will be September, and this is a good month for sailing. The winds calm down, and the sea settles. You know experience is a virtue. So, prepare everything to travel to Gran Canaria as soon as possible. Better today than tomorrow."

"As you wish, Your Eminence."

The bishop arrived in Gran Canaria on an old caravel, without incident, accompanied by good winds and calm seas. Upon setting foot on land, he said to his personal secretary:

"It seems we've made peace with Neptune, Miguel. You can't complain about the magnificent weather we've had. I even enjoyed the sailing, which is rare for me."

"Yes, Your Eminence, in the end, you were right; September is a good month for sailing."

***

Upon arriving at the episcopal seat, the bishop instructed his secretary to arrange a meeting with the inquisitor as soon as possible, as the trial was scheduled to begin in a few days.

The next morning at ten o'clock, the meeting between the bishop and the inquisitor took place at the episcopal seat.

The inquisitor entered the office and, after requesting permission, sat down. The prelate raised his head and said:

"I know it's surprising that I've called you for such a particular matter, especially concerning a renegade awaiting trial for heresy."

"Yes, Your Eminence. I'm still wondering why a bishop would take such interest in this matter and even come all the way from the island of Tenerife to inquire about it."

"My interest stems from my Christian conscience. I know the accused, Mr. Pérez, and I would like, within the limits set by the current laws, to act as the defense attorney for the accused Simón Romero Arráez, better known as Alí Simón or Alí el Canario."

The inquisitor shifted uncomfortably in his chair. The idea of a bishop wanting to defend a renegade, who was also a renowned corsair in Algiers, was beyond belief. He had never heard of such a thing.

"The proceedings are underway, Your Eminence, and a public defender has been assigned. It wouldn't be normal to change attorneys at this stage of the process."

The prelate smiled, stood up, and said calmly, hands clasped behind his back:

"I know the defendants have rejected the public defender, and I'm confident they'll accept me as their attorney."

"But, Your Eminence, the fact that they rejected the public defender is not grounds for assigning you as their defense attorney. Moreover, it's highly irregular for Your Eminence to present yourself like this, without prior notice, as their defense attorney. It's unheard of."

"Yes, I admit it's not usual, but I have my reasons, very powerful ones, for defending these two defendants, even though I know the accusations are very serious and challenging to refute. However, I would like to be present at the trial as their defense attorney, and I believe it's possible, Mr. Pérez."

"Possible, indeed, especially coming from the highest representation of our Holy Mother Church in these islands. I won't be the one to oppose such a request, but I'll need it in writing, Your Eminence."

Bishop Bartolomé García Ximénez de Rabadán knew it was unusual for a bishop to act as a defense attorney, but he also knew it was possible. That's why he had made the request.

"Thank you, Mr. Pérez. I won't forget this act of Christian charity and flexibility, which others might have outright refused."

"Know, Your Eminence, that the prosecutor has established the charges, and the defendants have admitted them, in a notarial confession. So, in the trial, you have little chance. You know that when the accused admit guilt, the matter is settled in a single session, and this is the case."

"Don't worry, I'm aware of those details, and I know it's difficult to argue against proven facts. But I want to try. For that reason, as a first step, I would like to speak with the defendants before the trial begins."

"Whenever you wish, Your Eminence. Both defendants are in the Castle of Mata."

"Perfect, I'll go visit them this afternoon."

"I'll give the necessary orders to ensure you can make the visit without any problems. If there's nothing else to discuss, I bid you farewell, Your Eminence. I have a multitude of files on my desk that I need to resolve before the year's end."

"Go with God, Mr. Pérez, and I reiterate my thanks for granting my request."

The inquisitor stood up and left the room. Shortly after, the secretary entered and said amazed:

"Did I hear correctly, Your Eminence? Will you be the defense attorney for Alí Romero?"

"Yes, Miguel, you heard correctly with those big ears of yours, always attentive to any murmur, even that of a fly."

"But, Your Eminence, do you think it's appropriate to expose yourself in such a way for a renegade who has confessed to being a Muslim?"

"At this stage of my life, dear Miguel, I care little for what others may say. I know that soon I'll be before the Most High. It is to Him I must give an account, and I know He won't reproach me for this Christian act of defending the defenseless. You know what the Lord Jesus Christ said, we must try to redeem the captive. That's what I'm doing, especially in this case."

" I've been in your service for many years, Your Eminence, and I can say that I know you very well. That's why I know that, despite this action of yours may seem like madness, it's done in good faith, and if there's any hint of sin in your behavior, God will forgive you."

"Oh, Miguel! I know my involvement in this case is not normal; I won't deny it. But never forget that the main mission of a Christian is to help others. That's what we're doing, esteemed secretary."

That same afternoon, the bishop, accompanied by his secretary, approached the Castle of Mata. They were escorted by two soldiers who led them to the dungeons of the building. The prelate descended the steep stairs to the cells with some difficulty. Two torches illuminated their path, while a strong odor of dampness and decay, accompanied by a slight breeze, made the torch flames dance.

One of the soldiers indicated the cell, opened it, and placed one of the torches on the wall. Then, the cell was illuminated.

The bishop approached the two defendants, waiting for his old eyes to adjust to the darkness. When he could finally see with some clarity, he said:

"Good afternoon, I am Bishop Bartolomé García Ximénez de Rabadán, and we haven't had the pleasure of meeting in person, Simón."

Alí Simón remembered the name he had heard and replied:

"Good afternoon, Your Eminence, for lack of a better greeting. In this dark cell, we don't know what day it is, or whether it's night or day. What brings you to us?"

"I know you've rejected the lawyer assigned to you by the Holy Office."

"You know better than anyone that the sentence is written and signed. Those accused of heresy and confessed renegades end up at the stake, and so will we. We don't need a lawyer for that."

"I'm here because I want to be your defense attorney, and if you permit me, I will be. The matter has been discussed with the presiding judge of the tribunal, and he hasn't objected to me acting as such."

Alí Simón couldn't believe what he was hearing, nor could he understand why the Bishop of the Canaries was in that cell with the intention of being his defense attorney.

"You'll have a very difficult task. The facts are clear and proven. There's little to defend," Alí Romero said with regret.

"I know. However, the case is not lost. The first thing you need to do is accept me as your attorney. Are you willing to let me represent you?"

Alí Simón looked at

his son and asked him:

"What do you think about having the bishop represent us?"

"Father, whatever you decide will be fine."

"Let's not speak more, Your Eminence. You'll be our attorney."

"If we agree on that, our first step will be for you to retract the statement you made before the notary, admitting to being Muslims and renouncing the Catholic religion. That statement would be the basis of my defense, and it would allow me to refute the accusations of heresy and Mohammedanism raised by the prosecutor."

Alí Romero fell silent and then said:

"We are Muslims, Your Eminence, and we're not going to retract our statement or make a declaration to the contrary."

"I thought you confessed to being Muslims to avoid torture and torment."

"You well know that I embraced the religion of Mohammed with an open conscience, and I haven't changed my mind. My son also thinks the same way."

"Don't forget, Simón, that if you acknowledge the Catholic religion as your own, you may avoid capital punishment and won't end up on a pyre. Life is the most precious asset a human being has."

"Your Eminence, put yourself in my shoes. Would you reject being a Christian under threat of being burned at the stake?"

"Of course not. However, this case is different, Simón."

"It's not different. You'll maintain your faith in Christ until the end of your days, and I'll maintain my faith in Allah until the end of mine."

"You're a man of strong convictions, and that's commendable. Know that if you maintain the statement you made, it will be very difficult for my defense to succeed."

"From the moment we were captured, we knew our situation would be complicated. We thought we might be used as bargaining chips to free a few captives in Algiers."

"In this case, Simón, it will be almost impossible. I'm convinced that the Inquisition tribunal has considered that aspect of the matter. But to judge and condemn a renegade who is also such a prominent corsair has an exemplary value they won't overlook. Hence my insistence that you rectify your initial statement. It's a way to nullify the exemplary nature of the sentence."

The corsair knew what the bishop was saying was true, but he was not willing to abandon his deep religious conviction.

"In this scenario, all we can do is entrust ourselves to God, Your Eminence. You to your God, and I to mine."

"Then let it be as God wills, Simón, and may He guide and enlighten us on this tortuous path."

The bishop left the prison pondering the matter, knowing that the defense of the corsair would be very complicated. It had a high chance of being a resounding failure. However, he wouldn't give up and would fight on..

The judgment

After a few weeks, Ali Simon was brought before the Tribunal of the Holy Inquisition, accused of heresy and Mohammedanism.

In the sole session held, the inquisitor entered the somber courtroom of the Holy Inquisition in Las Palmas with great solemnity. The defendants stood before the tribunal that would judge them. The first to speak was the judge of the tribunal, who stated:

"We are gathered here to address an accusation against Simon Romero Arraez, born in this place. At this moment, we also judge his son, who goes by the name El Kaid Romero. They stand accused of heresy and Mohammedanism. The accused has stated that his name is Ali Simon Romero Arraez and that he is the consul of the Basha of Algiers. It has been proven that the accused have renounced the Holy Catholic and Apostolic Religion. The floor is yours, Mr. Prosecutor."

"In the confession made by the accused before a notary," began the prosecutor, "it has been demonstrated that the accusations raised by this prosecutor correspond to the truth. If necessary, we will provide the witnesses needed to support the facts presented, but considering the defendants' confession, I do not believe the testimony of these witnesses is necessary. In any case, I will reiterate the question to the accused if they ratify their notarized statements. With the court's permission, I proceed to ask the question. Do you affirm what was stated in the notarial record in which you renounced the Catholic religion and remain faithful to the Mohammedan religion?"

"We indeed maintain what was stated before the notary," said Ali Simon.

"Let it be noted in the record what the accused has said. I have no further questions, Your Honor."

"The Most Illustrious Bishop Bartolome Garcia Ximenez de Rabadan has the floor."

The bishop rose slowly and, with difficulty, as if searching for the right words, spoke:

"With the permission of Your Excellency," he addressed the accused in a very measured tone, "I am aware of what has been stated in this tribunal because it has been brought to my attention in recent days. I am aware of the gravity of your statements, which even cause me pain and repulsion as to any good Christian. The prosecutor's accusations have a more than sufficient basis that I will not dispute here. What this tribunal does not know is that I have known the accused for some years, as have many captives. I had the opportunity to correspond with the defendant for a while. In those letters, I pleaded with the accused to return to the bosom of our Holy Catholic Religion, but he rejected such an offer. However, the situation in which we find ourselves is very different, Simon. The accusations being made against you in this act are extremely serious. I do not know if you are aware that you could end up turned to ashes in the burning stake behind the Convent of Santo Domingo or die in a galley."

"I am aware, Your Eminence, and I remember well the letters we exchanged regarding the captives I had in my service," Ali Simon stated.

"Part of this tribunal is unaware, and I state it here for the record, that you are a good Christian," the bishop continued.

"What are you saying, Your Lordship? A good Christian does not renounce his religion by embracing the religion of infidels," the inquisitor said indignantly.

"I know what I am talking about, Your Honor, let me explain," the prelate replied calmly.

"But this defendant has confessed before this tribunal that he is a renegade from the Catholic religion, and you know that the confession of guilt is considered full proof for condemnation," the prosecutor responded.

"I know, Mr. Prosecutor, I am aware of the gravity of the statements made by the accused in this tribunal. However, I have the moral obligation to present to you what I believe may aid in the absolution of my defendant. For that reason, I insist that this man is a good Christian who hides his soul under the religion of infidels because he had no other choice. He has lived among the Muslims for a long time and has not been able to prevent their evil influence. God is my witness to what I say, and so am I, Your Honor."

"Please explain yourself, Your Eminence. But know that your arguments, though weighty and deserving of the utmost consideration, will not change the opinion of this tribunal because the accusations against these defendants are very serious, and the formal acknowledgment of them is more than sufficient," the inquisitor warned.

"That is what I will do, Your Honor. Some years ago, I became aware that many Canarian families had relatives who had been captured in Barbary and made slaves by a Berber pirate who called himself Ali Simon and who was born in these lands. That Ali Simon is the accused being tried by this Holy Tribunal. After many difficulties, I managed to contact him through some personal letters. In that correspondence, I repeatedly begged him to grant freedom to the Canarian slaves. Later, I learned that he provided them with enough money to buy their freedom, thus preventing them from being sold as slaves, and he welcomed them into his home until they could repay the loan. From the knowledge of this circumstance, I insisted through some letters that he release the Canarian slaves under his custody. In late December 1686, I received the pleasant news that the accused had forgiven the debt to the slaves who, happily, returned safe and sound to the Canaries. I present to this tribunal the letter and testimonies of the freed captives, who would be willing to testify if this tribunal deemed it appropriate."

"You have a particular interest in this case, Your Lordship. Forgetting that the defendant is an infidel, who has renounced the Christian faith and has acknowledged it before this tribunal, that is grounds for an unequivocal condemnation," the inquisitor insisted with a stern expression.

"Undoubtedly, the facts are indisputable, but I insist, beneath the facade of a convinced infidel, hides a good Christian, and the facts prove it. Certainly, he may be condemned for his acts of piracy, but not for heresy, because his acts are of a manifest and overwhelming Christian charity," the bishop stated.

"I do not doubt that the release of those slaves was an act of Christian charity, but we are not judging that act here; we are judging the act of apostasy from the religion with which he was baptized. That is the act, that is the sin, and that is why he will be condemned. And if we add to this his activities of piracy over so many years and the harm he has done to the Crown of Castile, we have sufficient evidence to impose the harshest sentence, which can only be to be burned at the stake to atone for his sins," the inquisitor pronounced.

"But I would like to..."

"There is nothing more to discuss!" the inquisitor interrupted. "The sentence will be read in this same act. Thus, with the invocation of the name of Christ, we judge, attentive to the records and merits of the said inquisitorial process and the indications and suspicions that arise against Simon Romero Arraez and son, that we must condemn them to be burned at the stake. Thus, we order the sentence to be carried out in grace of the eradication of the proven heresies and apostasies before this tribunal."

The inquisitor rose without addressing the bishop and left, accompanied

by the other member of the tribunal, visibly angered, while the secretary drafted the sentence.

Ali Simon did not lose his composure as the bishop approached him and said:

"I will try by all means to ensure that the sentence is not carried out; I will petition for clemency."

"I appreciate it. You have done what you could. Do not involve yourself further in this matter because it will harm you. The Holy Inquisition has much power, as you know, and its tentacles reach the most unsuspected places."

"It is already harming me. I will draft that letter requesting clemency and that the punishment be commuted to imprisonment."

"My fate is written," Ali Simon said, looking him in the eyes and thanking him for what he had done for him and his son.

***

The next day, the bishop drafted the letter requesting clemency and handed it to his secretary to send to the tribunal. His secretary read it and then commented:

"You were aware that nothing could be done, Your Eminence, and you did what was in your power to prevent the condemnation that was decided before the trial began. You insist again and expose yourself again defending Simon Romero. Why do you do it, Your Eminence?"

"For the same reason he freed his captives, out of Christian charity, Miguel. That man, even if he swears he is a disciple of Allah, has a Christian heart, and in that, no one, not even the Holy Inquisition, will change my mind. The facts are there, the witnesses say it and swear it on the Bible. If not for the renegade, they would never have returned to their land. Those are the facts. Neither that man nor his son should die in the fire; perhaps they should pay their sentence for engaging in piracy, but not for confessing to be Muslims."

"With age, you are becoming very lenient and forgetting the principles of the Christian faith, Your Eminence."

"The only principles I follow are those of Our Lord God, which often stray from those established by our Holy Inquisition, which only see the precepts they have established over these last centuries. Jesus Christ forgave a prostitute and even those who nailed him to the cross. Remember his words: 'Father, forgive them, for they know not what they do.' Send the letter, Miguel, although I know what the response will be."

"I will deliver it in person, Your Eminence."

"Thank you, Miguel."

The Holy Tribunal replied, confirming the sentence it had dictated. So, on that same day, he ordered his secretary to arrange a meeting with Ali Simon to communicate the final sentence.

The bishop arrived in the late afternoon with his faithful secretary, and, as before, they were escorted by two soldiers. One of the soldiers opened the cell. The bishop entered alone and asked:

"How are you?"

"They treat us well, better than when we arrived. The treatment has improved, and so has the food. Perhaps it is because we have as our lawyer and friend the Most Illustrious Bishop of the Canaries, and that is worth its weight in gold."

"Having me as a defense attorney did not spare you from the maximum penalty," he said with regret. "That is why I have come, to inform you that the tribunal has rejected the request for clemency, which, on the other hand, was to be expected."

"We have not helped much with our defense either, but to think that the tribunal would have compassion for having freed a few captives was wishful thinking."

"A declaration of abjuration of the Muslim religion would have helped us."

"I know, Your Eminence, but perhaps they would have made us confess our supposed crimes with a good series of torture sessions, and in the end, it would have been the same."

"Perhaps. The truth is, there is no turning back. The sentence is final and will be carried out in a few days. Is there anything I can do for you?"

"I would like to see my parents and introduce them to their grandson."

The bishop remained silent for a few seconds and then said:

"Your father died three months ago, and your mother has been bedridden since your father died. According to what I have been informed, she is very ill. I thought you knew, Simon. One of your brothers is taking care of her, but I don't think he can come here. I am very sorry."

The corsair sighed, put his hands to his face, and said:

"I would have liked to see them one last time. I haven't seen my mother since I left over thirty years ago. I received a letter once a year from my brother Gaspar telling me how the year had gone. It's a shame. In the end, all you have left is family."

"If you want, I can tell your brother to come and visit you. It is not allowed, but I can arrange it, Simon. I still have some influence."

"No, let it be. Just tell him we are well, that Allah protects us, that he keeps taking care of our mother, and thanks for fulfilling our agreement."

"I will tell him only once, if you change your mind and want to return to the Catholic faith, I will be willing to come and confess you before the sentence is executed."

"Thank you, Your Eminence, for caring about us, but we will be fine."

"May God, whoever He may be, welcome you into His glory," said the bishop. Then he left the cell and went back to his seat.

Ali Simon remained with his son without saying anything, plunged into total darkness. Finally, his son, saddened, said:

"It seems this is our end, father, and we will die in the fire."

"There is no use in complaining, son. We will face this situation with courage and bravery because it is all we have left."

"I don't want to die, father," El Kaid said, sobbing.

"Come here, son, come closer and hug me. I will tell you that story I used to tell you when you were a child, do you remember? The one about the giant fish who wanted to be a small fish."

"Yes, father, of course I remember. Tell me."

"Once upon a time, there was a giant fish who wanted to be small. It was so big that when it surfaced, it looked like an island, and its shadow darkened the bottom of the sea..."

Believe in miracles

After a few days, Bartolomé García learned the date set for the execution of the two Barbary pirates. He knew it was unjust because, despite his past and present as a pirate, Alí Simón did not deserve to die at the stake. He paced in his study until his secretary entered and said, "The ship is scheduled to depart for Tenerife in two days, Your Excellency, and you seem to show little urgency in boarding it. Know that if we miss it, we'll have to stay for another week to ten days, and I know you wanted to return as soon as possible."

"I am still aware of the days and hours, Miguel. I have my mind on another matter that concerns me more than missing that ship."

"Are you not dwelling on the corsair matter? You know nothing can be done. The sentence is final and will be carried out in two days. Not even a miracle will save him from the stake. Inquisition judgments are immutable, Your Excellency."

The bishop knew this, but he wasn't thinking about the sentence; he was seeking a more drastic solution.

"You have the virtue of reminding me of what I already know, Miguel. Besides, you know miracles exist. If it weren't for them, you and I would be with God the Father. I need not remind you of the times we've escaped certain death."

"Yes, Your Excellency, I know miracles exist," he said, recalling the storms they had narrowly escaped on most of their voyages.

"Do you remember the general who was guarding Simón Romero?" he asked, looking out the window at the ocean.

"Yes, I remember."

"And do you recall his comment about his three sons who were held captive in Algiers?"

"Yes, perfectly."

"I would like to have an interview with him today."

"What are you thinking, Your Excellency?"

"That our Lord Jesus Christ continues to show us the way, dear Miguel. However dark the night, the light of a candle can illuminate our path."

"Can't you give me a hint about what's on your mind?" asked Miguel with great interest.

"No, bring me the general. I'll inform you of the details later if necessary. Go! Hurry and fetch the military man, time is against us."

***

The bells of the cathedral were chiming twelve when the secretary knocked on the prelate's office door and asked, "May I come in, Your Excellency? General Goez is here."

"Please, let him in."

The general entered and approached the desk, standing at attention. "Good morning, Your Excellency."

"Please, have a seat, General Goez. You must be wondering why I summoned you to the episcopal headquarters."

"Yes, I am unaware of the reasons, but I am here to serve you in any way I can."

"I know you have three sons held captive in Algiers, and I would like to hear the details of your case."

The captain shifted in his seat, his features hardening. The matter of his sons saddened and angered him to the point of sleeplessness.

"Yes, they have been in Algiers for two years. They are twenty, nineteen, and seventeen years old. They were captured north of the island of Lanzarote when coming from Cadiz. I've tried to free them, but they demand a lot of money, and you know the soldier's pay doesn't go far. I've sought help from the Trinitarians, but they focus their efforts on those without resources. I curse those corsairs, and may God have no mercy on them, Your Excellency. If I'm honest, I don't understand how you could agree to defend those infidels who spread fear and terror across the seas."

"I understand and share your pain, General Goez, but we're not here to discuss the reasons for my defense; we're here for something else."

"I don't understand, Your Excellency."

"Do you know who Alí Romero is?"

"Yes, I do. I paid close attention to his words during the trial."

"Then you'll know he's a very important and influential person in Algiers. A close friend of the dey of Algiers and, moreover, a very wealthy man."

"I don't see where you're going with this, Your Excellency," said the confused general, wondering why he was there.

"You're an experienced military man, with many friends in this town, many of whom owe you favors."

The military man slowly rose as he glimpsed what the priest was suggesting.

"Please, sit down, General Goez. Let me finish, then you can leave, but first, hear out my proposal."

The general sat and said, "I'm listening."

"The point is, I don't want the renegade corsair and his son to die at the stake because they don't deserve it. I believe they should pay for their sins in prison, perhaps until they die."

"I listened to your arguments," the general interrupted.

"Let me finish, General. I've tried to appeal for clemency to spare them from the death penalty in favor of life imprisonment. However, the Holy Tribunal did not grant my request, and the sentence will be carried out unless we intervene."

"Intervene? Preventing such a just sentence from being carried out?" asked the general, almost shouting.

"General Goez, I'm going to outline my plan, then you can assess it, and if you disagree, we'll drop it. But if I don't present it to you, I'll never have peace of mind."

The bishop watched as the general gritted his teeth, looking at him with fury, eager to leave the office as soon as possible.

"There's a caravel scheduled to depart for Tenerife the day after tomorrow, and on that same day, at sunset, the sentence is set to be carried out. My plan is for you to extract the renegade and his son from Castillo de Mata and take them to the caravel, which will transport them to Algiers. I'll give you a letter to Alí Romero stating that the price of their release is the freedom of his three sons and the Canarian captives held in that city."

The general Goez asked incredulously, "And how do you know this renegade will fulfill his part of the plan?"

"Don't ask how I know, General, but I am convinced he will. That corsair is a good Christian. As you know, he freed five captives without asking for anything in return. Why wouldn't he find a way to free his sons and the rest of his countrymen?"

The general's face relaxed because the bishop was offering him the only possibility of having his sons with him. No one had given him such a realistic solution to his problem.

"What do you think? Is it possible to carry out the plan I've outlined?" the bishop asked, noting the change in General Goez's attitude.

"It's possible. I have good friends who won't hesitate to help me because they know the torment I've been living with for two years. I only have one doubt, Your Excellency."

"Tell me."

"In case the renegade corsair doesn't fulfill his end, what do I gain?"

Bartolomé García expected that question and replied, "I'll commit in writing to fundraising campaign for the release of your three sons. I've done it before, and I assure you I'll raise the necessary funds, but I'm convinced that Simón Romero Arráez will keep his word. What do you say? Do you accept?"

"Your Excellency, you're a representative of the Holy Mother Church in a very particular way. I never thought you would participate in an action like this, let alone be devised by a high representative of the Catholic institution."

Bartolomé García Ximénez de Rabadán knew that what he was doing was beyond the established bounds of the law, but he also knew he had no other path to follow, and that was the only one he could take.

"Then, do you accept?"

"Yes, I accept, Your Excellency."

"You have a day and a half to organize the escape. Don't worry about the caravel; it's anchored in the Bay of Las Isletas. Tomorrow, a boat will be waiting for you on the beach, and it won't leave until you arrive with the corsairs. Don't worry about the ship's captain; he's entirely trustworthy and will tell a very credible story that no one will doubt."

"For my own sake, I'll do everything in my power. The freedom of my sons is above morals and laws. May God forgive me!"

"God forgives you, my son. In case you need help, don't hesitate to let me know. Go, we have much work to do."

The bishop watched as the general rose and quickly left. He called his secretary and said, "Prepare a carriage; we're going to the caravel."

"Are we leaving, Your Excellency? I haven't had time to pack."

"No, Miguel, we're not leaving. I need to speak with the captain of the caravel."

"I don't understand what's happening, Your Excellency," he said, confused.

"There's nothing to understand, Miguel. You just need to take me to the ship. On the way, I'll explain what's going on. Don't worry about a thing."

Along the way, Bishop Bartolomé García Ximénez de Rabadán recounted point by point the plan they were about to execute and General Goez's involvement.

The secretary fell pensive, then asked, "Are you aware, Your Excellency, that we're committing a crime

?"

"The thin line of justice today may be here and tomorrow, there, dear Miguel. I know where my head is, and I know this action is illegal, but I have no choice but to act in this way to save the life of a man who doesn't deserve to die burned alive at the stake. I need not tell you that I count on your support and discretion."

"I'm a tomb, I see, hear, and speak no evil, Your Excellency. Even if I think this isn't the correct way to act, I could never betray you."

"I expected nothing less from you. Loyalty is a very important virtue in these times and situations like the one before us. You have been a faithful secretary, but also a loyal friend."

After negotiating with a fisherman and paying him with some coins, he agreed to approach the caravel and inform the captain that they were waiting for him on the shore.

When he was on the beach, the bishop approached and told him about the plan that was underway. The sailor listened attentively, and when the prelate finished, he said, "I have no objection to taking those passengers to Algiers. I assume the renegade will pay me there, but if he doesn't, who will cover my travel expenses, Your Excellency? And I know you would cover any expenses incurred, but I would prefer some form of upfront payment as a guarantee. Put yourself in my shoes."

The bishop smiled. No one wanted to lose in this risky gamble he was making. He was the only one willing to lose. In a way, he couldn't expect any response other than doubt about implementing such a far-fetched plan.

"Don't worry, you're absolutely right. This world turns, and you never know what will happen tomorrow. Take this," he said, taking off the solid gold ring from his right ring finger. "In case the renegade doesn't fulfill the agreement, the value of this ring will cover the expenses. Is that sufficient assurance?"

The ship's captain was dumbfounded by the immense gold ring topped with a large red stone offered by the prelate.

"Your Excellency! I didn't mean this kind of guarantee. The episcopal ring cannot be a form of payment."

The secretary looked at the bishop with wide eyes, as if he were about to pop out of their sockets, not quite understanding what he was doing and not knowing if, for some reason, he was losing his mind.

"Don't worry, it's not the first time I've had to use the material goods of the bishopric to deal with pecuniary debts from my pastoral work. So take it; it's all I can offer. If the renegade fulfills his end of the bargain, you can return it to me when you return to Tenerife."

"I don't think it's appropriate. However, if Your Excellency agrees to offer me the ring as a guarantee, then I must also agree, don't you think?"

"Let's not talk about it anymore. Take it and keep it safe; that ring is worth more than its weight in gold, and besides, I have a great fondness for it."

"Don't worry, I'll guard it like gold."

They waited for the captain to move to the caravel, and when they had lost sight of him, the secretary said resignedly, "We're once again without a ring, Your Excellency."

"Not for long, Miguel. The material goods of the Church must be used to solve the problems of the bishopric, and this is one of them. Besides, I know Simón Romero will take care of all the debts incurred by his release."

"From this plan you've set in motion, there's something I still don't know, Your Excellency."

"Ask, Miguel, ask."

"Does the renegade know that he will be released and transported to Algiers tomorrow?"

"No, he doesn't know anything. He'll learn the details when he's at sea and safe. That's when he'll realize that Christians also pay their debts when necessary. He did a great deed without asking for anything in return. Now we return the favor. It's time to go back, Miguel. I'm very tired. The remnants of that poison are collecting their debt very quickly."

The secretary helped the bishop into the carriage, and when they were ready, they set off for the city.

Upon arriving at the episcopal headquarters, the prelate lay down to rest, looking up at the ceiling of his room, thinking that he could no longer do more than he had done for the corsair and that, from that day on, his fate was in the hands of God or Allah.

***

At dawn, just a day before the scheduled execution, a commotion stirred Ali Simon and his son from their sleep. They heard the creak of their cell's rusted iron gate opening and saw a light pierce the darkness of their chamber. A gravelly voice with a pronounced French accent whispered:

"Come, we have little time. A ship departs before dawn for Algiers, and you must board it."

"But how is this possible?" Ali asked in astonishment.

"You have good friends, sir, and many influences, whether you believe it or not."

Ali glanced at his son and said, "It seems our luck is beginning to change, son."

"I can't believe it, father. Who could our benefactor be?"

"I don't know, son, but I always told you we must never lose hope."

They obeyed without protest. Outside awaited a carriage that would take them to the Bay of Las Isletas, where the caravel awaited them to sail to Algiers. The Frenchman instructed them in a low, heavily accented voice:

"Lie down in the back of the carriage. I'll cover you with a blanket and then with these sacks of fruits and vegetables. Keep quiet during the journey."

The carriage set off, its two lanterns barely illuminating the path. The corsair and his son remained silent during the journey, listening only to the rattle of the cart. Upon reaching Santa Catalina Beach, they heard the Frenchman's voice and felt him removing the sacks of fruits and vegetables, followed by the blanket.

"You can come out now. We've arrived."

Ali Romero and El Kaid emerged from their hiding spot and got off the carriage. There they were met by the ship's captain, who said:

"Quickly. We have no time to waste. As soon as you board, we'll set sail for Algiers."

They boarded the boat, the captain hoisted the lateen sail, took the helm, and pointed the bow toward their vessel.

When they were in the middle of the sea, Ali Romero asked the captain:

"Can you tell me who our benefactor is?"

"When we're sailing safely on my caravel, I'll tell you."

As dawn broke, the ship unfurled its sails and set course eastward. Ali Simon walked toward the stern and remembered the day, that dawn, when he left his beloved land forever at the age of sixteen. Who had pulled the strings to secure his release? He had a faint idea of who might have orchestrated the plan to free him, but he couldn't believe it.

After more than three hours of sailing, with Gran Canaria's shores out of sight, the caravel's captain approached him and said:

"Now we are out of danger. Your benefactor asked me to give you this letter. He also told me that once you read it, I should destroy it."

Ali Simon took the missive and began to read.

Dear Simon,

I hope that, if you are reading this letter, you are well and on your way to Algiers, your home. During the journey, you may have wondered who your benefactor is, although I'm sure you had some idea of who arranged your release. But you know better than anyone that everything has a price, and your liberation has one, both for you and for me. Although my price will be paid before God the Father, for only He can judge me.

You are aware that there are still many Canarian families with their loved ones waiting to be released in Algiers. One of those tormented families is that of a Cádiz general stationed in this city, who has three of his sons imprisoned in the capital you are heading to. He has moved heaven and earth to free his sons, but after two years, he has achieved nothing. I contacted him to propose a plan, which was nothing other than your freedom in exchange for the freedom of his three sons and the Canarians from this city who are in Algiers. At first, he was hesitant because he said, who guaranteed that a renegade would keep his word after gaining freedom? I replied that you would fulfill the pact because I know you are a man of honor and, although you may not believe it, you are a good Christian despite being devoted to the prophet Muhammad. In the end, we sealed the secret pact of your liberation; I speaking on your behalf and he on his.

This military man, thank God, is a man of great determination, with much influence and many friends who owe him some favors. He devised a very clever plan to make it appear that it was the work of a Frenchman, whom I assume you know, by an unknown name and half-Algerian, who, with funding from the dey of Algiers, had hired a group of men to free you.

You must be wondering why a bishop has risked his reputation to free an infidel condemned by the Holy Inquisition. The reason is that I know you are a good man despite your piracy activities that go against all orders of justice, and you will pay when you are before God. I told you in person, and I'll say it again: you had a gesture worthy of God's forgiveness. But the courts of the Holy Inquisition, most of the time, lose sight of God the Father's magnanimity, and their obscurity prevents them from seeing the path of Divine Justice's enlightenment.

I could not allow a man who had made such a generous, such a Christian gesture, to end his days burned at the stake.

Attached to this letter is the list of Canarians who are captive in Algiers and the names of the general's sons. Don't forget to pay the captain what is due, and be generous because few would have done what he did.

In short, dear Simon, now you know why you are heading toward your beloved Algiers. I hope God guides you to the end of your days and keeps you and your family safe.

Gran Canaria, September 20, 1689

After finishing the letter, he smiled. He hadn't been wrong; his suspicions were correct. His son, who was beside him, asked:

"Who has been our liberator?"

"Bishop Bartolomé García Ximénez de Rabadán. Remember that name, son. Thanks to him, we have been reborn."

"I imagine our liberation will come with a price, father."

"Yes, but what is priceless is what the bishop did. First, he publicly exposed himself to defend a renegade and his son before the Inquisition, and then he devised a magnificent plan to set us free. We must fulfill our part of the deal."

"And what is that, father?"

The corsair recounted the details of what he had to do to fulfill his part of the agreement, and his son smiled; it was the fairest thing.

***

Upon docking in the port of Algiers, he approached the captain of the caravel and said:

"I don't know how long it will take me to find General Goez's sons. I don't even know if they are in this city. I offer you my home for rest. You are my guest, and my home is yours."

"I appreciate it, but my ship is my home, and I am accustomed to living in it."

"Wait two days. In that time, I hope to find the general's three sons. If I find them, I will return and deliver them to you. If not, I will return in the same manner and reimburse you for the expenses incurred for the outbound journey as well as the return."

"I will wait here. I need to replenish our supplies for the return journey. I would also like to obtain safe conduct, like the ones you give to the Trinitarians, to allow us to return without any trouble."

"Don't worry about that detail. I had already thought of it. You will have that safe conduct signed by the dey."

That same day, he located General Goez's three sons. The two youngest were serving as servants to an Algerian merchant, and the eldest was found sick and wounded in the Baths of Algiers.

He brought them to his palace and attended to them properly. He decided that the two youngest could travel, but the eldest had to postpone his return until he was fully recovered.

That same night, after a good bath and a hearty meal, he wrote a letter to Bishop Bartolomé García Ximénez de Rabadán:

Esteemed Excellency,

I hope that upon receiving this letter, health is your faithful companion.

I have no words to thank you for what you did for me and my son, risking your reputation to keep us safe. I will be eternally grateful to you.

I want to inform you that I have found General Goez's three sons. Two of them will depart tomorrow on the caravel that brought us to this city; the other, the eldest, will have to stay for some time because he is not fit to travel. When he recovers from his injuries, I will send him to Gran Canaria. I have explained the situation to the two younger sons, and they have agreed to leave, although it was quite a task to convince them. They did not want to leave without their elder brother. Thanks to the elder intervening and persuading them to see reason.

Regarding the rest of the captive Canarians, it will take me some time to organize their journey, but rest assured that I will also fulfill that part of the agreement.

I have also generously paid the captain of the caravel for the services rendered, and he was more than satisfied.

With nothing more to say, I hope that God and Allah take care of you and reward you for the good you are doing for the faithful of the Canaries.

Algiers, October 2, 1689

The next day, he went to the port with the general's two sons, boarded the ship, and on the deck, he said to the captain of the skull:

"Deliver this letter to Bishop when you can. Here is a bag with fifty gold coins that will be more than enough to cover the expenses incurred for this journey and the safe conduct signed by the dey of Algiers. I hope you won't need it. I would also like to thank you for agreeing to bring us here; few would have taken such a risk. If you speak with General Goez, thank him on my behalf. Tell him that as soon as I can, I will send his eldest son to Gran Canaria, and while he is staying at my house, I will take care of him as if he were my own son."

"I will deliver the letter to the bishop and look for the general to convey your message. As the bishop said, you are a man of your word and have more than fulfilled your part."

"As the Spanish saying goes, 'A grateful heart has its memory.' Something I learned a long time ago was to pay my debts, especially this kind of debt. You will have a friend here —said Ali Simon.

"Thank you. In these times, and given what I do, it's very helpful to have a friend in this port."

"Have a safe journey, and may Allah be with you."

Ali Simon watched as the caravel disappeared into the horizon and remembered Bishop Bartolomé García Ximénez de Rabadán and

General Goez. He took a deep breath and thanked Allah for keeping him alive.

Epilogue

In early November, when Bishop Bartolomé García Ximénez de Rabadán was resting on the island of Tenerife, his secretary entered his office with a letter in hand and a small black cloth bag.

"Here's the episcopal ring and a missive from your corsair friend. It was delivered by the caravel captain," the secretary said.

"At last, it seems they are fulfilling the commitments made. General Goez and our captain came through," remarked the bishop.

"It appears so, Your Excellency. You have an extraordinary persuasive ability because the plan to free the renegade was quite convoluted, and I thought it would never come to fruition."

The bishop couldn't agree more. He recalled the implementation of the plan and felt satisfied because it had worked from start to finish.

"Yes, so much so that the inquisitor had serious doubts that a Frenchman sent by the bey of Algiers could carry out such an ambitious plan. He told me there must be highly influential people behind it. I don't know if he was referring to me, I suppose so. Thank God, General Goez intervened, convincing him with compelling arguments supported by the testimony of five witnesses who corroborated his statements. Let's see what Simon Romero has to say. I hope he has also fulfilled his part," said the bishop, taking the letter and putting on his spectacles to read the text of the missive clearly.

He read it slowly. Then he smiled and said, "The corsair also fulfilled his part. He located the general's sons and embarked them all except the eldest, who was very ill. They must already be in Gran Canaria. He also paid our captain and is in the process of gathering the Canary captives for their release. What do you think, Miguel?"

The secretary smiled and said, "You have a keen eye for seeing into people's souls, Your Excellency. I told you so before."

"Perhaps, and only perhaps, Simon Romero would have been a great figure in this land, a great military man, a great merchant, or who knows, a great conqueror. But life's circumstances led him to become a famous corsair with a very Christian heart, more so than some who attend Mass on Sundays and holy days. I only wish for him to return to the fold of Father God someday."

He picked up the episcopal ring and put it on. Then he handed the letter to the secretary and said, "Keep it with the others, Miguel. I want to finish with this last text to rest a bit from my pastoral work. I am old and very tired, and I can almost feel death's breath on my neck."

"But what are you saying, Your Excellency? You have much life ahead of you."

The bishop struggled to rise, went to where his secretary was, and said, "You know that's not true, Miguel. I am deteriorating like a plant lacking water. The poison given to me by that son of Satan has done its job well. It has been eating away at my entrails like a cursed parasite almost without me noticing. Today I am aware of it, my dear friend. My days are numbered. However, I am not afraid of death. I only want to rest with the Most High. It is time."

"Don't think about that, Your Excellency. Finish the text. Then I'll prepare one of those infusions you like so much for you to rest."

He approached the window of his office, looked up at the sky, observed it carefully, and said, "They say a comet is approaching, which, on moonless nights, can be seen in the distance, and in fifteen days, it will be clearly visible. Also, a lunar eclipse will accompany me. Two prodigies that will lead me hand in hand to death, dear friend."

"For God's sake, Your Excellency! Stop mentioning the grim reaper!"

He returned to his desk, sat down, and said, "At least we have done good, or we have tried, despite the difficulties we have encountered along our way. We will meet the Lord with a record full of good deeds, Miguel. We have earned a place in heaven. Well, my friend, prepare that infusion for me; I want to go to sleep soon."

"Of course, Your Excellency, I'll bring it right away."

The bishop pondered that his life was nearing its end. However, when God called him into His presence, he would go with a clear conscience and the satisfaction of a job well done.

***

Ali Romero fulfilled his word. He gathered the Canary captives in Algiers, paid their ransom, and chartered a ship to take them to Gran Canaria. Along with them, the eldest son of General Goez would also embark.

Afterward, he spoke with his son to determine if he still intended to pursue privateering because it was a matter of great concern to him. So, a day after lunch, he remarked:

"I still believe you could take charge of our commercial ships. You have experienced firsthand what it means to be a corsair and the dangers it entails."

The Kaid looked at him and then said:

"I have been thinking a lot about that, father, and I believe you are right. I will take care of those ships, but only under two conditions."

"Tell me," he said with satisfaction, as if relieved of a burden.

"I want to travel one or two times a month on those ships and be the absolute head of the business."

"Perfect, son. That's what I wanted to hear. Now I can focus on resting and living life. I have long felt like I am living on the edge of a dagger. Besides, your mother wants me to spend more time by her side, and she is right. I have left her alone for many years, and it's time for me to fulfill my duties as a husband. However, you know I will be by your side for whatever you need."

"I know, father, and I will keep that in mind. Your experience and influence are worth their weight in gold, and it would be foolish not to take advantage of them."

"I trust you won't hesitate to ask me. Conscious ignorance only resides in fools, sons. So, ask when you deem it necessary. You know

I'll be there. This afternoon, we'll go to the port to organize your first commercial voyage, and tomorrow I'll request an audience with the bey to inform him that you will be the ultimate head of the family business."

"How will the bey take your retirement? You're a very important man to him."

"He will take it well because my best man will replace me, don't worry about that. My relations with the bey are excellent. We are very good friends. He will be delighted that you are taking over for me; in fact, he hinted at it once. He told me I was getting old, and when we were arrested, he insisted I give up privateering. In the end, I listened to him. I want to rest, son."

Ali Simon lived for many years. Some say he departed this world in 1691 due to a severe lung condition; others claim to have seen him in the redemption of Algiers in 1723, selling a batch of captives from Black Africa.

This is the tale of Ali Simon, a Berber corsair.

Don't miss out!

Visit the website below and you can sign up to receive emails whenever Moisés Morán Vega publishes a new book. There's no charge and no obligation.

https://books2read.com/r/B-A-BOUDB-ZVWPD

BOOKS2READ

Connecting independent readers to independent writers.

Also by Moisés Morán Vega

El primer escalón. Una selección de mis primeros relatos.
Historias de un esquizofrénico que no quería serlo pero que lo era.
Chat
El otro planeta
El Tatuaje
Un grado
El alambre mágico
Transfiguración
Jinámar Connection
Salvar al lagarto Tamarán
La Prometida
La sonata del pianista
Éxtasis
Mi Facebook después de muerto
K-70: Las aventuras de una tortuga majorera
¡Muerte al Borbón!
Pagarás por tus pecados
El coleccionista de puzzles
El cráneo
Entre dientes
Gracias por su visita
La oportunidad
Cóctel de Microhistorias terrenales
El origen competitivo de los botes de Vela Latina Una aproximación
histórica

Alí el Canario. Un corsario berberisco
Medio minuto para morir
Saduj. Caso I
No sin agua
Salvar al lagarto Tamarán. La culebra californiana
Poemas del ayer
Evolución deportiva e histórica de los botes de vela latina en Las
Palmas de Gran Canaria: 1876-1962
Saduj. Caso II. Internos
Caminar hacia la salud
Teatro reunido
Ali the Canary. A Barbary corsair

About the Author

BiografíaMoisés Morán Vega nació en Las Palmas de Gran Canaria el 20 de junio de 1965, en el barrio de Escaleritas.Ingresa en la Facultad de Educación Física y Deportes, donde se doctora en Educación Física con la tesis Análisis praxiológico de la situación motriz en competición de los botes de vela latina en Las Palmas de Gran Canaria (ULPGC 2005) y, posteriormente, cursa el Máster en Gestión Deportiva por la Universidad de Las Palmas de Gran Canaria.En el año 2007 se vuelve a interesar por la escritura de forma intensiva, escribiendo en su blog poesías, microrrelatos y relatos de diversa temática. Dos años más tarde, en el año 2009 gana el Primer Premio de Narrativa Breve Episodios Insulares convocado por la editorial Cam-PDS con el cuento juvenil, La Sima.En la actualidad es funcionario de la Comunidad Autónoma de Canarias y miembro activo de la Asociación Canaria para la Edición (NACE).BibliografíaNovelaHistorias de un esquizofrénico que no quería serlo, pero que lo era, 2010.Chat, 2013.Conexión Jinámar, 2014.Medio minuto para morir, 2015Alí el Canario, 2015Saduj. Caso I 2016Narrativa infantil y juvenilLa Sima, 2011 (Relato ganador del primer Premio de Narrativa Breve Episodios Insulares convocados por la editorial Cam-Pds en año 2009).Ali Romero. La historia de un corsario berberisco, 2011.Víctor, el caracol con un solo cuerno al Sol, 2012.Rocky y las tres cucarachas, 2012.El alambre mágico, 2013.Salvar al lagarto Tamarán: 2014.K-70: Las aventuras de una tortuga majorera, 2014.Alí el Canario. Un corsario berberisco. 2015Teatro"Gracias por su visita", 2015"Ganar, ganar", 2015"El testamento", 2015

Read more at https://elpatiodeloscangrejos.blogspot.com/.